Moral Abdication

Moral Abdication

On Consent to the Obliteration of Gaza

Didier Fassin

Translated by Gregory Elliott

VERSO

London • New York

This updated English-language edition published by Verso 2024
Originally published as *Une étrange défaite.*
Sur le consentement à l'écrasement de Gaza
© Editions La Découverte 2024
Translation © Gregory Elliott 2024

1 3 5 7 9 10 8 6 4 2

Verso
UK: 6 Meard Street, London W1F 0EG
US: 207 East 32nd St, New York, NY 10016
versobooks.com

Verso is the imprint of New Left Books

ISBN-13: 978-1-80429-967-8
ISBN-13: 978-1-80429-969-2 (US EBK)
ISBN-13: 978-1-80429-968-5 (UK EBK)

British Library Cataloguing in Publication Data
A catalogue record for this book is available from the British Library

Library of Congress Control Number: 2024945013

Typeset in Sabon MT by Hewer Text UK Ltd, Edinburgh
Printed and bound by CPI Group (UK) Ltd, Croydon, CR0 4YY

Moral Abdication

On Consent to the Obliteration of Gaza

Preface

From time to time, language dies.
It is dying now.
Who is alive to speak it?
               Fady Joudah, 2024

Consent to the obliteration of Gaza has created an enormous gulf in the global moral order. Retrospectively, the events which have unfolded in Palestine since Hamas's murderous attack on 7 October 2023, and the reaction to them in many of the planet's halls of political and intellectual power, will doubtless appear in the harsh light of their true significance. More than an abandonment of part of humanity – something of which international realpolitik has afforded many recent examples – history will record the support extended to its destruction. This acquiescence in the devastation of Gaza and the massacre of its population, to which must be added the persecution of the inhabitants of the West Bank, will leave an indelible trace in the memory of the societies that will be accountable for it. Following the rout of the French army in 1940, Marc Bloch wrote *Strange Defeat*, an uncompromising analysis of what had led to it. That defeat was military; today's is moral. It calls for an examination that must be carried out as lucidly as the French historian's, even if the context and issues are very different and even if the ethical divisions go much deeper.

An examination, then, of what led to a situation where, for political leaders and intellectual personalities in the principal Western countries – with rare exceptions such as Spain – the statistical reality that the lives of Palestinian civilians are worth several hundred times less than the lives of Israeli civilians, and the claim that the death of the former is less worthy of being honoured than that of the latter, have become acceptable; where demanding an immediate ceasefire in order to stop the massacre of children after more than 12,000 of them have already been killed, and so many others burned, amputated, traumatized, is denounced as an act of antisemitism; where demonstrations and meetings demanding a just peace are banned and people who refer to the history of the region are sanctioned; where, without independent confirmation, most of the mainstream Western media quasi-automatically reproduce the version of events relayed by the camp of the occupiers, while incessantly casting doubt on that recounted by the occupied; where state bodies, scientific institutions and university authorities impose silence on voices calling for the laws of war and international humanitarian law to be applied, while allowing free rein to those who flout them; where criticism of a government composed of far-right ministers giving speeches that dehumanize a people whose very existence it denies is equated with incitement to hatred; where so many of those who could have spoken, not to say stood up in opposition, avert their eyes from the annihilation of a territory, its history, its monuments, its hospitals, its schools, its housing, its infrastructure, its roads, and its inhabitants – in many cases, even encouraging its continuation. Such an inversion of the values proclaimed by Western societies, such a political dereliction, such an intellectual collapse demand examination.

The notion of consent probably requires some clarification. There are two distinct dimensions to it. The first is passive: not opposing a project, whose realization is thereby facilitated. The second is active: approving that project, whose realization is thus supported. In the case of the war on Gaza, the two dimensions are combined. When the UN Security Council declines to impose a ceasefire because of a veto by one of its members, or when the governing body of a higher education institution rejects the possibility of a vote condemning the destruction of universities and the murder of their professors, they passively consent in the first instance to the continuation of the massacre of the Palestinian population and the devastation of its territory, and, in the second, to the continuation of the crushing of the Palestinian education system and academic world. On the other hand, when heads of state line up in Jerusalem to affirm Israel's unconditional right to defend itself, or, when their governments send it massive quantities of weaponry, bombs and planes, they actively consent to no limits being imposed on retaliatory action and to additional resources being supplied to execute it – even when, in order to justify the killing of civilians, Israeli leaders and military figures publicly state that there are no innocents in Gaza. Remarkably, following the recognition by the International Court of Justice (ICJ) that there was a real risk of a genocide which had to be prevented, a shift occurred in some of the support from active to passive consent, but without any interruption in the dispatch of matériel. Throughout the war, however, a number of Western states have done more than consent. They have prevented those who defended the right of Palestinians to live in dignity, or simply to live, from expressing their views, accusing them of inciting hatred and apologizing for terrorism, arresting them on university campuses or barring them from entering European territory.

The paradox is that this moral abdication by states has been justified in the name of morality. European countries, it was said, had a historical responsibility towards Jews and must guarantee their security. The 7 October attack was a monstrous act threatening the very existence of Israel. Thus, the Israeli Defence Forces' (IDF) riposte became not only inevitable, but also legitimate. As to the death of Palestinian civilians, obviously that was regrettable, but it was to be regarded as collateral damage that the Israeli army was doing its best to avoid. The destruction of Gaza and part of its population was essentially a lesser evil for the sake of eliminating a greater one – namely, the destruction of the Jewish state on which Hamas was intent. In these circumstances, to speak of crimes being committed by the Israelis attested to the most suspect form of racism: antisemitism. This was especially true if genocide was invoked to refer to the massacre of the Palestinian population, for it was intolerable that the descendants of a people who had been the victim of the greatest genocide should be accused of perpetrating one. Good conscience was thus on the side of those supporting the collective punishment of the Palestinians. In short, not only were values inverted, but the very foundation they rested on became unstable.

'From time to time, language dies', writes the Palestinian poet Fady Joudah. 'It is dying now. Who is alive to speak it?' In the numerous exchanges I have had over these last months with people who do, or do not, share my view of what consent to the obliteration of Gaza means, two things have emerged: not only has the space for speech been restricted by the threats that hang over it, but there are no words to express what is taking place. All were conscious that, stunned and powerless, we were witnessing a major event in contemporary history whose moral consequences, political fallout and intellectual implications would be considerable. But the language to describe it seemed somehow dead. Or, rather, an attempt was underway to induce its death by imposing a vocabulary and grammar of the facts, by prescribing what must be said and condemning what must not be said, on pain of being singled out for public disgrace, ostracized from polite society, relieved of one's responsibilities, removed from one's institution, deprived of an income, stripped of a prize, excluded from a conference, subjected to a police inquiry, even summoned to appear before a court. This policing of language, which was also a policing of thought, was fuelled by denunciation by colleagues, professors, citizens and community organizations that demanded sanctions for the offenders. Restoring freedom of speech, demanding a debate about words, defending a language that might make the world more intelligible, had therefore become a necessity.

This necessity became all the more imperative when, following the ICJ's ruling that the commission of a genocide in Gaza was 'plausible', history began to be rewritten. The most embarrassing traces of encouragement of war crimes in the name of the 'right to self-defence' were erased. Those who had supported the bombardment of Gaza and its blockade began to declare the Israeli government accountable for the so-called humanitarian crisis it had caused. Having censured the voices calling for a cessation of hostilities, they suddenly declared themselves in favour of it. Having been bellicose, they evinced compassion. Having practised censorship, they minimized it. They distanced themselves from Israeli government communications. In the midst of this revisionism, it was necessary to collect evidence to contribute, modestly, to building an archive of something that will leave a deep wound in a century already marked by wars and massacres.

These wars and massacres are indeed invoked by some to relativize the singularity of the obliteration of Gaza. They legitimately point to Congo and the Kivu, Sudan and Darfur, Ethiopia and Tigray, Turkey and the Kurds, Russia and the Ukrainians, Myanmar and the Rohingya, China and the Uighurs, and more. Each of these situations is tragic. Some have involved a greater number of victims than in Gaza. But none of these wars and none of these massacres have elicited such unwavering support from Western governments and so systematic a condemnation of any who denounce them, while the scale of the devastation and the intent to erase are beyond compare.

'Sometimes it is better to be lost for words', wrote the British philosopher Brian Klug, two months after 7 October. 'Perhaps we should hold our tongue until we find words that approximate to reality – the brutal human reality of suffering, grief, loss, and despair . . . There are times when we need to stop talking in order to start thinking – thinking politically.'[1] To this prudent injunction, the Saudi-born anthropologist Talal Asad replied: 'Yes. But perhaps in the present situation in which deliberate cruelty is being done and shamelessly denied, what is necessary is not only thinking but also speaking and acting morally.' And yet, he added, 'How one can do that is more difficult than it might appear . . .'[2] This difficulty makes it only more crucial to try. If not now, when?[3]

1

The war being waged on Gaza was triggered by a bloody incursion into southern Israel on 7 October 2023 by the military wing of Hamas and members of several other Palestinian organizations. The attack caused the death of 1,143 people, including 695 Israeli civilians, 36 of them children, in kibbutzim and at a music festival, 71 foreigners and 376 military personnel.[1] According to testimony from survivors and investigations by Israeli journalists, some of the civilians were probably killed by fire from their own army.[2] At least 222 people, including children, were taken as hostages to Gaza with a view to exchanging them for Palestinian prisoners.[3] A forty-eight-minute film made by the Israeli army, involving a montage of sequences filmed by the attackers, surveillance cameras, and first-aid workers who arrived on the scene after the assault, and recording the murder of Israeli civilians and soldiers by members of Hamas, has been shown to selected foreign journalists and politicians, without being made publicly available.[4]

The acts of violence committed by the assailants on 7 October have given rise to contradictory statements and intense controversy.[5] Thus, after being repeated for weeks in the media and political circles, including by the US president, accounts reporting forty babies beheaded and a pregnant woman ripped open, which inflamed the sense of horror and the desire for revenge, have been officially invalidated.[6] Similarly, the testimony of an Israeli nurse to the effect that he had seen two partially undressed adolescents showing signs of sexual aggression in a kibbutz was contradicted by a video taken on the spot by a soldier, after having likewise been circulated by major international press outlets.[7] As for the investigative article by a leading US daily paper, reporting on its front page the rape of a young Israeli woman during the rave on the basis of a statement by a figure known for spreading far-right conspiracy theories, the facts have been contested by the family, who said they had been manipulated by the journalists.[8] Nevertheless, despite the difficulties met with in confirming the facts – in particular because of the Israeli authorities' refusal to cooperate with the UN's independent international commission on sexual violence in conflict situations, the impossibility for its members to meet any first-hand witness, the ban on doctors who cared for survivors talking to experts, and the absence of medico-legal evidence of the alleged violence – the commission's report, produced at the end of a brief and difficult mission four months after the attack, indicates 'reasonable grounds to believe' that acts of sexual violence were committed by Palestinian fighters.[9]

Hamas's deadly raid caused a profound trauma in Israel and for many Jews around the world. The number of fatalities is by far the highest since the birth of the State of Israel in 1948. Media coverage of the sexual abuse committed caused a stupefaction commensurate with the descriptions and commentaries it elicited from political leaders, military figures and journalists.[10] Alongside the shock occasioned by the scale of the killing, and by the sense of the threat hanging over the Israeli population, was anger at a government that had failed in its duty to protect its citizens, by ignoring warnings about the risk of such an attack and prioritizing its grip on power; and furthermore had encouraged the growth of Hamas as a counterweight to Fatah, thereby reducing the chances of a political settlement of the conflict.[11] For some, the indignation mounted when it transpired that freeing the hostages was not a government priority and was actually secondary to the objective of obliterating Gaza.[12] Even so, the majority of the population supported Operation Swords of Iron, with an opinion poll conducted in late October by Tel Aviv University indicating that nearly eight out of ten Jewish Israelis approved of their army's action in Gaza, while only 2 per cent regarded the IDF's bombing campaign as too intensive.[13] Although few in number, the latter, opposed to the collective punishment being meted out to Palestinians, merit a mention. For example, five days after the death of her brother, killed during the assault, Noi Katzman declared, 'The most important thing for me, and also for my brother, is that his death will not be used as a justification for killing innocent people.'[14]

There have been arguments about how to categorize the events of 7 October. While killing civilians is a war crime and can even be characterized as a crime against humanity in certain conditions, the significance of Operation al-Aqsa Flood, as it was named, remains the subject of debate. For some, often said to be pro-Israeli, it was a pogrom, the victims having been brutalized and executed because they were Jews. For others, generally classified as pro-Palestinian, it was an act of resistance in response to oppression at the hands of an enemy army. The first version casts the aggression as an anti-semitic act, authorizing some to even speak of genocide. The second accords it the political meaning of a rebellion against the occupation of one part of Palestinian territory and the suffocation of the other. The first interpretation is the sole legitimate one for most governments in the West, who regard the attack as what the French president called the biggest antisemitic massacre of the twenty-first century.[15] The second is condemned, even proscribed, by these same governments and by a number of academic institutions and media outlets, prompting charges and summonses by the police and trials for apologizing for terrorism.[16] But it is frequently accepted in many countries of the Global South.

Among analysts who regard Hamas's operation not as a killing spree against Jews, but as a revolt against

Israeli oppression, there are differences over how to interpret the violence.[17] Two frequently cited articles illustrate these tensions. For the US historian and editor Adam Shatz, the aim of Hamas's 'offensive' was 'to reassert the primacy of the Palestinian struggle at a time when it seemed to be falling off the agenda of the international community'.[18] The attack on Israeli military posts thus corresponded to 'classic – and legitimate – guerrilla warfare against an occupying power', and the images broadcast of it 'gave rise to understandable euphoria among Palestinians'. But the murder of civilians was 'a blood-drenched bacchanalia' that the author compares to the 1955 Philippeville uprising in Algeria, construing it as a 'vengeful pathology' and denouncing 'the ethno-tribalist fantasies of the decolonial left' enthused by the assailants' heroism. For the Palestinian philosopher Abdaljawad Omar, one should speak instead of 'hopeful pathologies'.[19] He criticizes intellectuals who sympathize with the Palestinians when they are 'tragic victims sinking graciously into their own abyss', but are outraged when they 'dare to rebel' against their oppressor, killing civilians in the process, while it is the Israeli army that has theorized and implemented, under the Dahiya doctrine, a strategy of massive destruction of civilian populations and their infrastructure as a mode of asymmetrical warfare. In short, while Adam Shatz, holding the act of Palestinian resistance to be legitimate, condemns the murder of Israeli civilians, Abdaljawad Omar, while not justifying it, underscores the lesser indignation of the Western world when it is

Palestinian civilians being murdered by Israeli soldiers or settlers. For both, what is at stake is articulating the moral issue of excess with the political issue of liberation. This is also what the Palestinian historian Tareq Baconi aims for when he writes, 'The worldview of Palestinian resistance fighters is that they are engaged in a justified war against a violent and illegal occupation that terrorizes them and their family members. Their adoption of armed struggle, in this particular context, draws on its own legal, political, and theological justifications.' He adds, 'Without justifying this resort to violence, one has to see and understand it from a center of gravity that is rooted in the Palestinian territories, not in the West.'[20]

The difference between the two readings of the 7 October attack – as an antisemitic pogrom or as an act of resistance – is frequently coupled with a difference in the role allocated to history in interpreting the events. The importance of mastering temporalities was strikingly expressed in George Orwell's dystopian novel: 'Who controls the past controls the future. Who controls the present controls the past.'[21]

For some, the starting point lies in Hamas's bloody incursion: there is no past. What is more, invoking history is suspect and reprehensible, because it seems to offer an excuse for the operation against Israeli civilians and soldiers.[22] Thus, every day the newspaper *Haaretz* publishes a news page online entitled 'Israel at War'. Using an identical formula, it recalls the 'context' – namely, that the country 'declared war after Hamas killed at least 1,200 Israelis and wounded more than 3,330 in a merciless assault' – simply adding that the conflict 'comes after ten months of the worst political and social crisis in recent decades, due to the government's judicial coup'. It makes no mention of the occupation of the Palestinian territories.[23] The same leitmotif has been taken up by the mainstream French media, print and audio-visual, citing the 7 October attack as the sole antecedent to the war in Gaza.

For others, the event is part of a long history beginning in 1917 with the Balfour Declaration, whereby the British colonial power stated that it 'viewed with favour the establishment in Palestine of a national home for the Jewish people', as recalled by the Palestinian American historian Rashid Khalidi in his account of the 'hundred years' war'.[24] Skipping over the creation of the State of Israel in 1948, many refer to a briefer history beginning in 1967 when Israel, on the morrow of the Six-Day War, rejected the UN resolution delimiting the Palestinian territories and occupied a growing area of them through colonization and militarization. This was anticipated by General de Gaulle, who declared immediately after the conflict that Israel 'is now organizing occupation on the territory it has seized. This cannot proceed without oppression, repression and expulsion, and without the emergence of resistance to it, which in turn it characterizes as terrorism.'[25] Out of a concern to introduce some historical perspective, in late October, when the bombardment had already resulted in the destruction of a quarter of the buildings in northern Gaza and the death of thousands of civilians, the UN secretary general attracted Israel's wrath by stating that while 'nothing can justify the deliberate killing, injuring, and kidnapping of civilians', Hamas's attacks 'did not happen in a vacuum', but followed 'fifty-six years of suffocating occupation'.[26]

The Palestinian American poet and psychologist Hala Alyan argues that there is something her dual activity has taught her: 'It matters where you start a narrative.' And she goes on: 'As long as we exist, we challenge several falsehoods, not the least of which is that, for some, we never existed at all.'[27] Yet the historical context has not always been denied by the Israeli authorities. In 1956, when a Palestinian Fedayeen crossed the border separating Gaza and Israel and killed the caretaker of a kibbutz, General Moshe Dayan, head of the Israeli military, declared during the victim's funeral: 'Let us not hurl blame at the murderers. Why should we complain of their hatred for us? Eight years have they sat in the refugee camps of Gaza, and seen, with their own eyes, how we have made a homeland of the soil and the villages where they and their forebears once dwelt.'[28] Naturally, this statement was intended not so much to justify an act of resistance as to legitimize reinforcing the border. But it established a historical link to a past of dispossession which the Israeli government and its foreign supporters now refuse to acknowledge.[29]

In fact, to start the present sequence of events on 7 October is not only to evade history, but also to confer a particular significance on the facts themselves, with

two crucial implications for those who defend this ahis-
torical view. Firstly, the violence committed in southern
Israel appears to amount to sheer savagery, as irrational
as it is unpredictable, on the part of members of Hamas.
This makes it possible to strip them of their humanity
and, using metonymic reasoning, to extend the discourse
of hatred and the logic of retaliation to all Palestinians.[30]
Secondly, the Israeli state is enabled to disclaim all
responsibility in the genesis of the events, whether by
dint of decades of oppression and suffocation of the
Palestinian population, or on account of the strategy
employed to boost the organization that inflicted this
ordeal on it.[31] These two logics – de-humanization and
denial of responsibility – account for the brutality of
the military response in Gaza.

Conversely, to invoke history, to recall the continuous
seizure of land in the West Bank, the constant evictions
from housing in East Jerusalem, the blockade of the Gaza
Strip, the raids in Jenin refugee camp, the limits on movement, the restrictions of liberties, the violation of rights, the
arbitrary arrests and detentions without charge or trial, the
death or mutilation of children and adolescents, the daily
humiliations and aggression suffered at the hands of settlers
and soldiers – this helps to understand how a situation that
has become unbearable can lead to a rebellion, since peaceful protest was ineffective in preventing the illegal extension
of settlements and military zones while Israeli repression
has become increasingly murderous in recent years, with a
record number of Palestinians killed by the army in 2022,
often in the absence of any confrontation.[32] In this respect,

the contrast is striking between the relative moderation of the IDF in the 2000s faced with non-violent mobilization by the inhabitants of the village of Budrus, near Ramallah, against the dispossession of their fields and the destruction of their olive trees in order to build a security barrier set to encircle them beyond the Green Line, and the atrocities perpetrated since the 2010s.[33]

The formula 'Israel–Hamas War', adopted by most mainstream Western media to describe events in Gaza after 7 October, is, in reality, doubly misleading. On the one hand, it does not take into account the fact that the conflict began well before that date. Without going back to the Israeli occupation from 1967–2005, or mentioning the deadly paroxysms of 2009 and 2014, there was constant violence in the years immediately preceding Hamas's attack, as shown by the brutal military response to the mostly peaceful demonstrations of the Great March of Return in 2018 and 2019, which caused the death of 214 Palestinians, including 46 children, and wounded 36,100, including 8,800 minors.[34] On the other hand, it masks the fact that the state of siege imposed since 2007, with its sanctions and blockade, targets all the inhabitants of Gaza, declared a 'hostile entity' by Israel. By preventing half a million workers from entering its territory, and significantly restricting trade in commercial products and the delivery of humanitarian aid, Israel has been asphyxiating the population.[35] According to the UN Special Rapporteur on the Situation of Human Rights in the Occupied Palestinian Territories, the siege of Gaza had transformed it 'from a

low-income society with modest but growing export ties
to the regional and international economy to an impov-
erished ghetto with a decimated economy and a collaps-
ing social service system'.[36] But to recall this history is to
expose oneself to the usual charge by political and
academic authorities, according to whom, in the words
of a former French president regarding terrorism, 'when
you start by seeking to explicate the inexplicable, you
are preparing to excuse the inexcusable.'[37]

Faced with this refusal of history, it must be recalled
that to understand is not necessarily to condone, and
that one can attempt to analyse an act even though one
condemns it. In this respect, one accusation is incessantly repeated against those who call for a ceasefire,
denounce the slaughter of civilians in Gaza, demand an
end to the blockade of the territory and the authoriza-
tion of humanitarian convoys, and call for the liberation of the hostages held by Hamas and the prisoners
incarcerated in Israel – all elements that are to be found
in most petitions and declarations: 'You don't say
anything about 7 October,' comes the retort. On the one
hand, this is frequently inaccurate, for most of these
interventions do refer to Hamas's attack, condemn the
violence, and bemoan its victims. On the other, this
criticism ignores the temporality of the facts, since one
can only demand a halt to a massacre when it is underway, not several months after it has occurred. Even so,
the accusation remains recurrent, especially against the
left and feminists.[38]

2

Adopting a historical perspective makes it possible not only to examine the ashes of the past, but also to look ahead to a potentially brighter future.

In particular, history clarifies the characterization of terrorism. Whereas it initially denoted practices peculiar to a state – those of the Terror during the French Revolution – today the term is exclusively applied to persons and organizations that attack a state. When operations conducted by a state aim to terrorize populations, they are no longer regarded as terrorist, but as pertaining to counterterrorism – even though the French historian Henry Laurens points out that they kill many more people than the acts classified as terrorist.[1] As the French political scientist Mathias Delori has highlighted, in order to justify counter-terrorism being more lethal than terrorism, its protagonists deny that they intended to kill innocents, whose death they present as collateral damage of a just cause, that of combating terrorism. Added to this asymmetry is another: from the viewpoint of those who define such categories, terrorism kills at home while counterterrorism kills abroad, which also explains the greater tolerance of the loss of life it causes.[2] But perhaps the most remarkable fact about what is called terrorism is the lability of the categorization. For, on the one hand, it allows certain states to criminalize their enemies, whose struggle is, however, recognized elsewhere as legitimate; while, on the other, it can be inverted over time in the world's moral conscience, with some of yesterday's terrorists becoming today's heroes.

In South Africa, the African National Congress (ANC), whose paramilitary wing uMkhonto weSizwe carried out a series of attacks that caused the death of members of the security forces but also civilians, was long regarded by the UK and US as a terrorist organization. By contrast, in most countries of the world it was seen as struggling against the oppression of the White supremacist regime. The ANC's founder and leader of its armed wing, Nelson Mandela, architect of the peaceful transition to democracy and the country's first president after the end of apartheid, featured on the list of terrorists drawn up by the US until 2008 – eighteen years after leaving prison and fifteen years after receiving the Nobel Peace Prize alongside F. W. de Klerk. Irgun, a paramilitary far-right Jewish organization likewise deemed terrorist by the UK and US, carried out assaults on British colonialists and massacres of Arab civilians, notably at Deir Yassin in 1948. Having become prime minister of Israel, its leader Menachem Begin signed a peace treaty with Egyptian president Anwar Sadat at Camp David in 1978 and, the same year, was rewarded with the Nobel Peace

Prize along with him. The Palestine Liberation Organization (PLO), which had been declared terrorist by most European countries after a series of violent acts largely against Israeli civilians, but which enjoyed the support of the socialist and non-aligned countries, was recognized in 1974 by almost all members of the UN as the legitimate representative of the Palestinian people. Its leader, Yasser Arafat, negotiated the Oslo Accords with Yitzhak Rabin in 1993, and together with him received the Nobel Peace Prize the following year. He was the first president of the Palestinian Authority.

The point is not to use history to relativize the violence of political organizations classified as terrorist by Western nations, yesterday or today. It is, rather, to conceive that they might be seen differently elsewhere in the world, and that their very status can change over time depending on the balance of forces they have succeeded in establishing in international relations.[3] One might think of the FLN, the National Liberation Front in Algeria; the IRA, the Irish Republican Army; or the FARC, Revolutionary Armed Forces of Colombia. These are formerly terrorist groups for some, liberation movements for others, which have participated, and are still participating, peacefully in the political life of their countries. Meanwhile, it is true that other entities, from Shining Path to al-Qaeda, have not taken this road. Thus, history cannot serve to predict what, in ten, twenty, or fifty years, the relations between the Jewish state and a future Palestinian state may be like, or the role that will be played in them by organizations which have, at one time or another, been designated as terrorist. History simply helps, in the light of the past, to rethink the present and sometimes to imagine possible futures.

There is a cruel but undeniable reality: the 7 October attack brutally put the question of Palestine back on the international stage, from which it had been excluded by Israel, the United States, most members of the European Union, and a growing number of Arab and African countries. The world lived with the incarceration and death of thousands of Palestinians, the illegal extension of Jewish settlements in the West Bank, the suffocating blockade of the Gaza Strip, the normalization of Israel's relations with the United Arab Emirates, Bahrain, Sudan and Morocco by the Abraham Accords (which were due to be completed by a treaty with Saudi Arabia), and the transfer of the US embassy to Jerusalem on land belonging to Palestinian families (a decision that contravened the principle of not creating diplomatic missions in the Holy City of three monotheisms). The violations of international laws and UN resolutions, the growing oppression of Palestinians by the Jewish state and progressive absorption of their territories in the Greater Israel were globally accepted. 'Among those in government in Israel, some believed that you could completely ignore the question of Palestine and normalize relations with the Arab countries as if it was business as usual', observed the Israeli writer and journalist Michel Warschawski, adding, 'They were seriously mistaken.'[4] The Western world shared this view. Who still seriously spoke of a Palestinian state prior to 7 October? Despite recognition of the latter by 138 of the 193 member countries of the United Nations, the Western world – with the exception of Iceland and Sweden – had until then succeeded in preventing the application of the international law that affirmed 'the right of the Palestinian people to self-determination and to independence', so as to achieve the creation of 'an independent, sovereign, democratic, contiguous and viable State of Palestine living side by side in peace and security with Israel on the basis of the pre-1967 borders'.[5]

On 22 September, two weeks before Hamas's attack, in a speech to the UN General Assembly, the Israeli prime minister displayed a map presenting a 'New Middle East' in which Eretz Israel had absorbed the West Bank and the Gaza Strip. This statement came after another, some months earlier, during his investiture as head of the government, when he proclaimed that 'the Jewish people have an exclusive and unquestionable right to all areas of the land of Israel – Galilee, the Negev, Golan, Judea and Samaria.'[6] For his part, during a lecture in Paris on 19 May delivered in front of a flag likewise representing Israel after its absorption of all the occupied Palestinian territories, the finance minister, who is also in charge of colonization, asserted that there was no such thing as Palestinian history or Palestinian culture, 'not even a Palestinian people'.[7] Recent events have tragically restored these territories to the map of the world and this people to the imaginary of nations. Contested by some and abandoned by others until only a short while ago, the possibility of a Palestinian state is now on practically all political agendas, even those of Israel's staunchest allies, albeit not without double-speak.[8] As the former president of the Israeli Sociological Society Lev Luis Grinberg formulates it: 'Palestinian resistance is in a catch: when it uses violence it is oppressed, and when it uses diplomatic negotiations it is ignored.'[9]

That the rebirth of the Palestinian question has been paid for in the massacre of hundreds of Israeli civilians and tens of thousands of Gazan civilians makes the years of inaction by Western governments, and the indulgence of numerous others in the face of ever more blatant Israeli violations of UN resolutions and Palestinian rights, particularly hard to bear.[10] The responsibility of the so-called international community cannot, indeed, be overlooked. The painful truth about the genealogy of the murderous attack of 7 October, its even more murderous consequences, and its political impact on the Palestinian cause, may be regarded as intolerable. It certainly is. But it is an attested fact, which explains why, a little less than two months the brutal incursion in the south of Israel, when more than 15,000 inhabitants of Gaza had been killed and Gaza City was reduced to rubble, nearly three-quarters of Palestinians affirmed that, for all the suffering they had endured as a result, 'Hamas's decision to carry out the offensive was correct' – even if support for Hamas and Operation al-Aqsa Flood was significantly lower among the inhabitants of the Gaza Strip than among residents of the West Bank.[11]

3

Words matter, especially when they have historical reso-
nance, political meaning and legal implications. On
29 December, the Republic of South Africa initiated
proceedings against the State of Israel at the ICJ in The
Hague for 'alleged violations by Israel of its obligations
under the Convention on the Prevention and Punishment
of the Crime of Genocide in relation to Palestinians in
the Gaza Strip'.[1]

It was not the first time that the word 'genocide' had
been used in the public arena in connection with the war
being waged by Israel. On 15 October, more than 800
academics and researchers from around the world,
specialists in political science, conflict studies and the
analysis of genocides, had alerted the international
community to 'potential genocide in Gaza', recalling
that the sixteen years of the blockade of the territory
had already been characterized as a 'prelude to genocide'.[2] On 19 October, nine UN special rapporteurs had
referred to 'a risk of genocide against the Palestinian
people' on the basis, in particular, of 'statements made

by Israeli political leaders and their allies'.[3] On 15 November, Palestinians had begun legal action against the US president and two of his ministers for 'failure to prevent and complicity in the unfolding genocide against Gaza'.[4] On 12 December, the International Federation for Human Rights, which brings together 178 organizations from 120 countries, expressed its alarm more assertively in a resolution by its international board on 'the unfolding genocide in Palestine', indicating that 'states that provide arms and political support are therefore complicit.'[5] On 26 January, four weeks after the case was brought, the ICJ, having heard the South African and Israeli arguments, delivered its ruling.

It must be recalled what the 1948 UN Convention on the Prevention and Punishment of the Crime of Genocide, ratified by South Africa and Israel, says. For some of those challenging its applicability in the present case seem unaware of its terms.[6] 'Genocide means any of the following acts committed with intent to destroy, in whole or in part, a national, ethnical, racial or religious group, as such', explains the text, which provides a precise list of such acts: '(a) killing members of the group; (b) causing serious bodily or mental harm to members of the group; (c) deliberately inflicting on the group conditions of life calculated to bring about its physical destruction in whole or in part; (d) imposing measures intended to prevent births within the group; (e) forcibly transferring children of the group to another group.' Punishment for one or more of these acts applies to those involved on any of the following grounds: '(a) genocide; (b) conspiracy to commit genocide; (c) direct and public incitement to commit genocide; (d) attempt to commit genocide; (e) complicity in genocide.'[7]

In short, recognition of this crime presupposes both acts and intent. As early as 10 November, the Israeli American expert in genocide studies Omer Bartov expressed concern that evidence of the latter in Israel heralded realization of the former in Gaza: 'My greatest concern watching the Israel–Gaza war unfold is that there is genocidal intent, which can easily tip into genocidal action.'[8] Scarcely two months later, in the eighty-four-page document it had drafted for the UN judicial body, South Africa established in detail that intent had indeed become action, drawing on six hundred sources. Firstly, there was considerable destruction, including of health and educational facilities, and mass crimes against civilians, through bombardment and a total siege that were depriving the population of food, access to water and the possibility of healthcare, while blocking access to humanitarian aid. Secondly, numerous statements by Israeli political leaders, military chiefs and other public figures attested to a project to flatten Gaza and annihilate its inhabitants. These facts and statements were systematically gathered by South Africa.

The facts are irrefutable. During a press conference on 22 December, UN Secretary General António Guterres stated that 'humanitarian veterans who have served in war zones and disasters around the world

– people who have seen everything – tell me they have seen nothing like what they see today in Gaza.'⁹ When South Africa drafted its document, less than three months after the start of Israel's military intervention in Gaza, 21,110 Palestinians had already been killed, 70 per cent of them women and children, added to whom were 7,780 missing persons decomposing under the ruins of buildings. According to US intelligence services, nearly half the bombs released on the territory were dropped blindly, while bombs weighing 2,000 pounds and killing or wounding people in a 360-meter-diameter area were loosed on densely populated areas. These two factors attested to an intent to decimate civilians indiscriminately. Every day, more than 100 children were dying, and it was estimated that more children had been killed in Gaza in the first three weeks of the war than in every year since 2019 in all the planet's other conflicts. During the mass evacuations imposed by the Israeli army, displaced persons had been targeted by soldiers, drones or bombs on routes that were supposed to be safe corridors.

Certain professions had been especially affected: 311 doctors, nurses and other health workers, 103 journalists, 209 teachers, and 144 UN personnel, humanitarian workers for the most part, had been killed in under three months. During this period, 238 attacks on health structures had been logged, in which at least 570 people were killed and a further 746 wounded among patients and displaced persons who had sought refuge in these buildings. Among the 55,000 wounded, 1,000 children had lost one or both lower limbs, and the use of white phosphorous incendiary munitions had caused severe burns. The fear and trauma caused by the bombing, the military presence, the forced displacement, and the spectacle of death and destruction had given rise to serious mental problems, above all among the youngest. Given the total or partial destruction of hospitals and clinics, the death of numerous health personnel, and the absence of electricity and medication, the wounded, the burned and the sick could scarcely any longer be treated and amputations were sometimes conducted without anaesthetic. On account of the damage to sea water desalinization plants through bombing and power cuts by the army, access to drinking water was reduced to one-tenth of the minimum threshold required in conditions of famine.[10]

Indeed, the total blockade imposed since the start of the war led to ever more profound food shortages. This situation was exacerbated by the devastation of cultivated areas providing local food supplies and the destruction of more than two-thirds of fishing boats. The population had thus become dependent on humanitarian aid, of which the Israeli army finally allowed the passage of a mere tenth of that required, and whose convoys had sometimes come under fire from Israeli soldiers. According to the UN, at the start of 2024 half a million people faced the highest level of food insecurity, deemed 'catastrophic', with a complete shortage of food, total exhaustion and famine. When rare foodstuffs did arrive in the Gaza Strip, the rush of starving inhabitants towards the distribution sites prompted melees and brawls, while

MORAL ABDICATION | 31

tanks and snipers sometimes fired on the crowd – as
occurred on 29 February for more than an hour during
the 'flour massacre', when 118 Palestinians were killed
and 760 wounded. Fourteen similar, if less deadly, attacks
had preceded this bloodbath.[11]

The humanitarian situation has been further aggra-
vated by Israeli accusations against the United Nations
Relief and Works Agency for Palestinian Refugees in the
Near East (UNRWA), by far the largest international aid
agency in Gaza, twelve of whose employees were accused
of participating in the 7 October attack. This led to a
suspension of financing by sixteen of the largest donor
countries, including the United States, Germany and
France, with no solid evidence from Israel of the involve-
ment of these workers, which even US intelligence agen-
cies considered unlikely.[12] The UN independent mission
chaired by Catherine Colonna issued its conclusions in a
fifty-four-page report published on 22 April 2024,
confirming that Israel had not provided any ground for
its accusations, attesting to the absence of antisemitic
language in UNRWA textbooks, praising the rigorous
neutrality of the agency's activities, and making a series
of recommendations for further improvement.[13] In reality, it seems that destabilization of the agency formed
part of an Israeli plan to 'eliminate UNRWA', whose aid
trucks have been banned from entering Gaza, with the
result, according to its director of planning, that 'simply
more people will die'.[14]

The verbal statements about Israel's project are no
less compelling than the facts. The Israeli historian Raz

Segal, who speaks of 'a textbook case of genocide', notes that it is rare for perpetrators to express their intention to commit genocide in so 'explicit, open, and unashamed' a fashion.[15] For, very soon, statements from the highest levels of the state indicated that Israel's military intervention in Gaza aimed at much more than the disappearance of Hamas – an objective regarded by most experts as unattainable. The whole territory and its inhabitants without distinction were the target. The list of quotations documented by South Africa is impressive: the prime minister enjoining soldiers to 'remember what Amalek has done to you', an allusion to the Biblical enemy whose 'men and women, infants and sucklings' Israel should, according to Scripture, 'kill alike'; the president announcing that 'an entire nation out there is responsible' and 'we will fight until we break their backbone'; the defence minister indicating that there would be 'no electricity, no food, no water, no fuel', since this was a war against 'human animals' and 'we are acting accordingly'; the minister of National Security clarifying that 'when we say that Hamas should be destroyed, it also means those who celebrate, those who support' its actions, because 'they are all terrorists, and they should also be destroyed'; the Energy and Infrastructure minister declaring that 'they will not receive a drop of water or a single battery until they leave the world'; the vice-chair of the Knesset announcing that 'we all have one common goal – erasing the Gaza Strip from the face of the earth'; a reservist major-general explaining that it was necessary 'to make Gaza a place that is temporarily, or permanently, impossible to live in' and that 'the people should be told they have two choices: to stay and to starve, or to leave'.[16] There are dozens more quotations from parliamentarians, journalists and soldiers repeating that there are 'no innocents' and there is 'no place for humanitarian gestures'. As remarked by the US lawyer and anthropologist Darryl Li, the strength of the case presented by South Africa consisted in this 'meticulous reconstruction of genocidal intent'.[17]

The ICJ was persuaded by the argument about both acts and intent, and its members, including the judge representing the United States, almost unanimously supported the order. Pending a final decision on the substantive issue, which will probably take years, in the measured language of what is primarily an order aiming to prevent 'a real and imminent risk of irreparable prejudice', it recognized that in light of the 'facts and circumstances' presented, the invocation of the Convention on Genocide and the measures proposed by the plaintiff were 'plausible'. Consequently, it was a matter of 'urgency' that Israel take all necessary measures to avoid the commission of the crimes indicated in the Convention, to punish those inciting them, and to allow the entry of international aid.[18] When the ruling was announced, the South African government issued a victory communiqué, the Israeli government denounced the charges against it as antisemitic, and Gaza's inhabitants expressed their disappointment that there was no demand for a ceasefire.[19] France, whose foreign minister had opined that to speak of genocide was to 'cross a moral line', diplomatically took note of the order and the injunctions issued, while recalling that the assertion of this crime required 'establishing an intention', as if he gave no credence to the plentiful evidence adduced by South Africa.[20] As for the United States, some weeks later it once again opposed a Security Council resolution for a ceasefire, liberation of the hostages and removal of the obstacles to humanitarian assistance, oddly arguing that such a resolution would hinder negotiations between the Israelis and Palestinians.[21] Making light of the judicial body's conclusions, both countries continued sending matériel to the Israeli army, France claiming that the munitions delivered were officially intended for re-export, without any checks being conducted on the truth of the matter, and the United States supplying arms worth several billion dollars, including thousands of the nearly one-tonne bombs used to destroy Gazan residential areas.[22] Several Western countries, notably Spain and Italy, stopped arms sales to Israel after 7 October; Germany, by contrast, increased its deliveries of matériel tenfold in the space of a year.[23]

Frustrating as it is for Gaza's inhabitants, who continue to be bombed and starved by the Israeli army, the ICJ's recognition of the plausibility of the commission of genocidal acts by Israel is nonetheless significant for the obligations it imposes, in principle, on the Israeli government, hanging over which is the possibility of a verdict of genocide, but also on the governments supporting it, which are beginning to be accused of complicity. As a consequence of the Court's decision, sanctions should have been envisaged in the event of non-respect for the terms of the order. Instead, after six months of war, more than 33,000 deaths, twice as many injuries, a population reduced to famine, and endemic child malnutrition, no Western country had seemed ready to risk them, with several even supporting the Israeli army militarily.[24]

As for the potential recognition of a genocide, it is a long process. Namibia is well aware of this.[25] The genocide of its Herero population by the Germans in what was South West Africa began in 1904, yet was only recognized by the German authorities in 2021, some 117 years later. After Germany's announcement at the ICJ that it would support Israel's unconditional right to defend itself, the Namibian president denounced Berlin's double standard: 'atonement for the genocide in Namibia, while supporting the equivalent of a genocide in Gaza'.[26] Linking the two events was all the more inescapable for Namibian observers in that the Herero, men, women and children, had themselves been exterminated both by the pitiless firepower of the German army and by famine and dehydration, as a result of the total blockade imposed on the gateways of the desert into which the population had been driven.[27]

The Israeli specialist on the Holocaust and genocide, Amos Goldberg, would not have been surprised either by the comparison, since in 2011 he had written in *Haaretz* a column in which he issued a warning: 'From the Herero and Nama genocide we can learn how colonial domination, based on a sense of cultural and racial superiority, can spill over, in the face of local rebellion, into horrific crimes like mass deportation, ethnic cleansing and genocide. The case of the Herero rebellion should serve as a horrifying warning sign for us here in Israel, which has already known one Nakba in its history.'[28]

4

The UN Special Rapporteur on the Situation of Human Rights in the Palestinian Occupied Territories, Francesca Albanese, is in no doubt about how to characterize the facts. Her report, presented on 25 March, was entitled *Anatomy of a Genocide*.[1] In twenty-five dense pages, containing 309 references, it furnishes the evidence to justify its title. Yet this official characterization, if it were to be confirmed, will only occur at the end of a protracted and difficult legal process. But, whatever the outcome, in which the balance of power between countries might prove more decisive than international law, the evocation of a genocide committed by a state founded by the UN in reparation for the greatest genocide ever perpetrated is a highly sensitive issue. 'It is a tragic lesson of history,' laments the sociologist Edgar Morin. 'The descendants of a people persecuted for centuries by the Christian and then racist West can become both persecutors themselves and the advanced bastion of the West in the Arab world.'[2]

In these circumstances, it is easy to understand the resistance of the Israelis and their allies to this recognition. Some have even reversed the accusation, with members of Hamas being equated with 'Nazis' and the 7 October attack being presented as a new 'Holocaust', while the Israeli ambassador to the UN presented himself in public with a yellow star on his jacket.[3] 'One way of understanding Israel', writes the American historian Gabriel Winant, 'is to say that it is a machine for the conversion of grief into power.'[4] Instrumentalization of the genocide of European Jews to justify the violence of the military response, and exonerate it in advance, has been subject to criticism, notably from the director of the Yad Vashem memorial.[5] The leap backward in time from Hamas's attack to the Wannsee Conference, from 7 October 2023 to 20 January 1942, skipping over more than eight decades of relations between Jews and Arabs in Palestine to justify the massacre of Gaza's population, is certainly a dangerous reconstruction of history – and not only for the victims. 'A genocidal war waged in the name of remembering the Holocaust can only offend and discredit that memory, with the result of legitimizing antisemitism', writes the Italian historian Enzo Traverso: 'We would then enter a world where everything is equivalent, and words no longer have any value.'[6] Voices were indeed raised, including among Israel's most loyal supporters in the United States, to warn that the country's image in the world would suffer lasting damage because of the devastation of Gaza.[7]

Meanwhile, the dominant strategy employed by the Israeli government and its Western allies to combat what they regard as a serious legal and political threat to the leaders of the Jewish state rests on two pillars: legitimizing the military operation conducted against the Palestinians, and discrediting criticism of it.

On the one hand, the intervention in Gaza and its methods have given rise to a rhetoric of denial based on three main arguments used by Israel and its supporters.[8] Firstly, following the 7 October attack, Israel has the 'right to defend itself' and any appeals for the protection of civilian populations are pusillanimous and hypocritical, masking a rejection of the effective exercise of that right.[9] Secondly, it denounces the utilization of women and children as 'human shields' by Palestinian organizations, which explains why its army destroys the hospitals and schools where the militants are said to be hiding.[10] Thirdly, it boasts 'the most moral army in the world', the proof being that the IDF gives advance warning by telephone of the targets it intends to strike, distributes flyers asking the affected inhabitants to leave, and creates humanitarian corridors to enable their evacuation.[11] Each of these arguments has been subject to detailed refutation.

The right of self-defence against an aggressor is certainly legitimate, but it also applies as the right of self-defence against an oppressor. In both cases, the deliberate killing of civilians is a war crime, even potentially a crime against humanity.[12] Also, while investigations carried out after the military operations of 2009 and 2014 in Gaza concluded that there was no empirical basis to the accusation of using 'human shields', such a practice would hardly make much sense in the context of the current intervention, given that the IDF indiscriminately bombs health and educational facilities on the grounds that there is 'no non-combatant population' in Gaza – which makes it pointless to try to hide in these buildings.[13] In fact, it has even been documented by Israeli journalists and a Palestinian organization that it was the IDF who used Palestinian civilians, including children, as human shields, sending them to search tunnels and buildings where they suspected that bombs might be hidden and forcing them to walk in front of the tanks in the streets to avoid being attacked. IDF officers justified this by telling soldiers that 'our lives are more important than their lives'.[14] Besides, according to a spokesperson for the Israeli army, the 'emphasis is on damage and not on accuracy'. This has resulted in massive strikes on residential areas where inhabitants had been instructed to take refuge – a tactic intended, as indicated by one intelligence agent, to 'create a shock' among the population, rather than to eliminate members of Hamas, who generally shelter in the tunnels dug under towns and cities.[15]

As for the ethics of Israeli soldiers, ample evidence, including from dozens of videos taken by military personnel themselves, reveal the forms of violence, humiliation and dehumanization they inflict on civilians who have been captured. Examples are stripping women and cutting their hair; undressing men and making them repeat, at gunpoint, chants against Hamas, praise of the Israelis, and sentences where they declare themselves their slaves; chaining a hospital medical director by the neck to walk him like a dog and make him eat from a bowl; broadcasting on social media the emaciated portrait of a child dead from malnutrition as the announcement of a sequel to the film *E.T.*[16] The discovery around the main hospitals of several mass graves containing hundreds of bodies revealed not only the presence of elderly persons, women and children still dressed in their hospital gowns, but also naked bodies, some of which showed signs of torture, while others had their hands tied.[17] Indiscriminate killings are not deviant acts, they are in fact authorized by commanders, and soldiers admit that 'there is total freedom of action', 'it's permissible to shoot everyone, a young girl, an old woman', and this even becomes entirely justified for men, since 'every man between the ages of sixteen and fifty is suspected of being a terrorist'.[18] For Israeli soldiers, displaying themselves in uniform with their weapons in front of destroyed buildings, or near prisoners in their underwear, has become disturbing proof of virility proudly exhibited on dating sites.[19] The military personnel posting obscene images accompanied by outrageous comments include some of the more than 4,000 French nationals enlisted in the Israeli army. One of them recorded himself in a tank announcing that 'we are going to massacre them, massacre them', against the background of a parody of a well-known song whose altered words are 'No more Arabs'.

However, the French government has refused to carry out investigations into their abuses, let alone initiate criminal proceedings.[20]

At the same time, thousands of Palestinians, including pregnant women and young children, are detained in overcrowded prison cells and the open-air cages of military camps. The Public Committee Against Torture in Israel has documented that several dozens of them have been killed and numerous others arbitrarily subject to physical abuse, degrading treatment, forced strip searches, and deprivation of medication, while the International Committee of the Red Cross, human rights organizations, lawyers and families are systematically denied visiting rights.[21] These practices of torture and degradation are not concealed. On the contrary, they can be the topic of reports on national TV channels, which thus publicize the spectacle of vengeance and satisfy the desire for punishment.[22] But not everything is shown to the Israelis. 'Have they heard about the prisoners whose hands and feet were amputated because of gangrene caused by handcuffs?' asks the Israeli journalist Hanin Majadli. 'Do they know that over the last six months, the number of prisoners who have died in Israeli torture camps is four times greater than the number of prisoners who died in Guantanamo over twenty years?'[23] The head of orthopaedics at al-Shifa hospital is among the numerous prisoners who have succumbed to their conditions of detention and torture.[24]

On the other hand, criticism of the Israeli intervention leads to accusations of antisemitism, with serious consequences. And yet in 2016 the International Holocaust Remembrance Alliance provided a 'working definition', adopted by all thirty-one member states, according to which 'antisemitism is a certain perception of Jews which may be expressed as hatred towards Jews', making it clear that 'criticism of Israel similar to that levelled against any other country cannot be regarded as antisemitic'.[25] However, among the examples of the latter given by the authors, several have been systematically wielded by communal organizations and Western governments to prevent any analysis of the historical circumstances of the birth of the State of Israel and the policies implemented in the Palestinian Occupied Territories. This instrumentalization of the definition has been condemned by the very legal scholar who was its principal author and by one hundred organizations, including Jewish and Israeli ones.[26]

According to the Indian writer Pankaj Mishra, if such an interpretation of the definition had been operative half a century ago, Jean Améry, the Austrian philosopher tortured by the Gestapo and sent to Auschwitz, and Primo Levi, the Italian writer likewise imprisoned in Auschwitz – both of them Jews, Zionists and Holocaust survivors profoundly attached to the existence of Israel – would have been treated as antisemites.[27] In fact, when, in the 1970s, they witnessed the development of an Israeli plan to conquer the whole of Palestine that relied on exploiting the genocide of European Jews in the capacity of victims; and then saw the invasion of Lebanon, while the Occupied Territories were subjected to increasing colonization, both men were highly critical.

In 1977, Améry wrote that, 'unless one is willing to compromise one's commitment to the unity of morality and enlightenment', the moment had come 'to chart on an imaginary moral map the limits of the solidarity that binds diaspora Jewry to Israel', referring in particular to the fact that Prime Minister Menachem Begin, founder of Likud, regarded the occupied West Bank as 'liberated'.[28] At the same time he underlined the importance of the 'pact of solidarity with the country', thus drawing a clear moral line between loyalty to the Jewish state and opposition to the Israeli government.

In 1984, Primo Levi observed that 'the role of Israel as a unifying centre of Judaism was in a phase of eclipse', which he hoped would be 'temporary', and that at the time 'the centre of gravity was to be found in the diaspora', which must remind Israelis to 'jealously guard the Jewish thread of tolerance'.[29] While reiterating his attachment to the Jewish state, he expressed his disquiet at the unfolding situation in the country with the rise to power of Defence Minister Ariel Sharon, stressing, two years after the Sabra and Shatila massacre, the need to 'withdraw from Lebanon' and 'withdraw from the West Bank and Gaza'. His critique of Israeli policy was thus accompanied by concern for the values abandoned by the State of Israel, to which he himself remained loyal.

Today, such distancing has become dangerous. Even when more moderately formulated, disavowal of Israeli policy and its war on Gaza brings down on those who express it charges of antisemitism not only in Israel, but also in a number of Western countries. It was precisely to counter this development that the Jerusalem Declaration on Antisemitism, signed by 350 international academic specialists in Jewish studies, proposed a more unequivocal definition and less problematic guidelines in 2020. In particular, the following were not to be regarded as antisemitic: 'supporting the Palestinian demand for justice and the full grant of their political, civil and human rights', 'criticizing or opposing Zionism as a form of nationalism', comparing 'Israel with other historical cases, including settler-colonialism or apartheid', and promoting 'boycott, divestment and sanctions, non-violent forms of protest against states'.[30]

Notwithstanding the Jerusalem Declaration, conflation of criticism of Israeli policy, or criticism of Zionism, with antisemitism remains the rule for Western governments, mainstream media and academic institutions. This has resulted in the democratic paradox that to criticize a government comprising far-right ministers, which promotes religious supremacism, fashions discriminatory legislation, rejects international law, and carries out massacres of civilian populations, is to expose oneself to the accusation of iniquity.[1] France has long rubber-stamped this conflation. Thus, in 2014, at the start of the war waged by Israel in Gaza, following an intervention by the French president extending his full support to the Israeli government, the Socialist foreign affairs and interior ministers published a column in the *New York Times* to assure readers that 'France is not an antisemitic country' and that 'the French government is firmly standing by the country's Jews', even when no particular incident could justify their declaration.[2] This 'communalization of the conflict' at the highest level of the state, which associates the struggle against antisemitism with defence of Israeli policy, while assuming that all French Jews automatically support this policy and that antisemitism is principally connected to the question of Palestine, has never been disavowed.[3] It took a further dramatic turn in 2019, when, at the annual dinner of the Representative Council of French Jewish Institutions, which defines itself as a Zionist organization, the French president declared that 'anti-Zionism is one of the modern forms of antisemitism', after having stated, contrary to the Jerusalem Declaration, that France intended to adopt a definition of antisemitism that would include anti-Zionism.[4] This assimilation is based on the allegation that anti-Zionism means condemnation of the existence of the State of Israel, whereas it is first and foremost a criticism of the way in which a certain interpretation of Zionism has fuelled the enterprise aimed at denying Palestinians' rights and occupying the whole of Palestine.

Several recent incidents have demonstrated how this conflation makes it possible to prevent debates and penalize those who organize them. The most significant event occurred during a meeting held at Sciences Po Paris on 12 March, at the instigation of its Palestine Committee.[5] It brought together students, researchers and professors, including Jews, to discuss, among other topics, the relations between 'Judaism and anti-Zionism' across the religious divide. Protests were heard in the amphitheatre when a member of the Jewish Students Union entered, because she was accused of taking photographs of people on previous mobilizations and sharing them on social networks, which resulted in the doxing of the students thus identified. News of this brief verbal altercation having been rapidly mediatized, the following day it elicited a reaction from the French president, who denounced 'unspeakable and intolerable' statements, referring to the fact that, according to an anonymous witness, the student had been called a 'Zionist' – something she herself said she had not heard. Within hours, a minister was invoking 'antisemitism' and the government spokesperson condemned 'the beginnings of separatism', while the prime minister deplored a 'downward spiral linked to a dangerous activist minority'. Accompanied by a sizeable police deployment, he visited the institution during a session of its governing body to announce that it would be taken in hand in order 'to guarantee republican principles'. A few days later, in an open letter, the heads of the institution's schools and departments, as well as elected representatives from their various bodies, expressed indignation at an 'interference' violating the 'basic principles of academic independence and freedom'. Meanwhile, a report of antisemitic discrimination had been submitted to the public prosecutor. However, not only would the term 'Zionist', were it to have been uttered, do little more than reiterate the position proclaimed by the association to which the student belonged, but thirty-seven Jewish students, shocked by 'exaggerated media and political hype', declared in a joint text that they had been 'well received and included as Jews for the duration of the event', in the course of which they had been able to calmly express their point of view.[6] This intervention by the government in an institution of higher education, prior to any checking of the facts, illustrates the dangerous game of amalgamating Jewish and Zionist, antisemitism and criticism of Israeli policy.

Such conflation is not peculiar to France, and the German authorities have practised it even more assiduously to stigmatize the rare public statements on the situation in Palestine. On 25 February, during the closing ceremony of the Berlinale, the filmmakers Basel Adra and Yuval Abraham received the Best Documentary prize for *No Other Land*.[7] Shot in difficult conditions due to threats from the Israeli army, the film depicts the resistance of the Palestinian inhabitants of Masafer Yatta in the West Bank to the plundering of their land, the destruction of their homes, and their eviction from the region. During their acceptance speeches, the two directors referred to the war in Gaza. 'It is very hard to celebrate when there are tens of thousands of my people being slaughtered and massacred by Israel in Gaza', the Palestinian Basel Adra admitted, calling on Germany to stop its arms exports to Israel. 'In two days' time we will go back to a land where we are not equal. I'm living under a civilian law and he is under military law', the Israeli Yuval Abraham said of his colleague, characterizing this situation as apartheid. In the hours that followed, the mayor of Berlin condemned their words as 'unacceptable' and 'antisemitic', and the representative of the Federal Government for Culture and Media referred to statements 'characterized by a profound hatred of Israel'.[8] In response, the Israeli director expressed his dismay: 'To demonize us, to devalue the term of antisemitism like that – how dare German politicians lecture an Israeli whose entire family either survived or was murdered in the Holocaust?' He added that such comments were putting him and his loved ones in danger.[9] Sure enough, following the attacks by the German authorities, he received death threats at home and gave up on returning to his country, his family having had to be evacuated from its residence in Israel. To denounce someone as being antisemitic because they criticize Israeli policy, or simply try to make a Palestinian voice heard, is heedlessly to expose them to retaliation.

An anecdotal but revealing fact indicates how the accusation of antisemitism can go to extremes. The Swedish face of the struggle against global warming, Greta Thunberg, has paid the price. Faithful to her principles of social and environmental justice, she publicized her solidarity with the Palestinians by appearing with activists carrying 'Free Palestine' and 'Stand with Gaza' placards, and demanding an 'immediate ceasefire', as well as 'freedom for all Palestinians and all civilians affected'.[10] The Simon Wiesenthal Center accused her of antisemitism and even of legitimizing the genocide of European Jewry – an accusation that took on an international dimension when it was relayed in the *Boston Herald* and *Der Spiegel* alike. One detail provoked particular indignation. In a photograph circulating on social networks, a plush toy octopus was positioned behind the young woman. This animal is reputed to soothe people who, like her, have an autism spectrum disorder. Yet some read its presence as a metaphorical evocation of Jewish influence in the world, as in late-nineteenth-century caricatures.[11] The attacks on Greta Thunberg intensified.

This emblematic episode reveals a dual phenomenon of appropriation of the meaning of symbols and criminalization of their users, which has served to discredit criticism of the military operation in Gaza. Thus, a charge of antisemitism was brought against French students who, to denounce the massacre of Palestinians, painted their hands red, as many others did on university campuses elsewhere in the world. Yet a link was swiftly made with the photo of a man showing off his palms covered in blood after he had taken part in the killing of Israeli soldiers in Ramallah in October 2000. The accusers seemed to ignore the way this sign has long been used in disparate political struggles to denounce lethal politics, from the dictatorship of Pinochet in Chile to the abuse of Aboriginals in Australia. In fact, just a few weeks before the French incident, it has even been employed on several occasions by Jewish Israelis protesting against their government's policy regarding the hostages.[12] More generally, the normalization of a charge of antisemitism for adopting any position against the war, or even for any critical analysis of the policy pursued by the Israeli government, generates censorship and self-censorship in Western countries.[13]

Firstly, numerous events have been prohibited. In France, among several similar bans, a lecture on the ICJ's ruling on the war in Gaza was called off at the University of Lyon 2 at the request of the Representative Council of French Jewish Institutions, which denounced it as conveying a 'message of hate'. In the same city the same organization had already attempted to cancel an exhibition entitled 'Gaza, Wounded Infancy' by the Palestinian photojournalist Mohammed Zaanoun, one of very few able to send out images of the war.[14] In Germany, amid a series of cancellations of artistic events, one of the biggest cultural centres in Berlin lost its annual state grant after organizing an event with the anti-Zionist group Jewish Voice for a Just Peace in Palestine, deemed a 'concealed form of antisemitism', whereas it actually involved commemorating the victims of both Hamas and the IDF in ecumenical fashion.[15] The Australian anthropologist Ghassan Hage and the American philosopher Nancy Fraser had their contracts rescinded by the Max Planck Institute of Social Anthropology and the University of Cologne, respectively, for condemning the massacre of civilians in Gaza.[16] Similarly, the Palestinian British surgeon Ghassan Abu-Sittah found himself refused entry to Germany, where he was due to participate in a conference on Palestine that was eventually prohibited by the Berlin police; and some weeks later, when he was invited to a symposium at the French Senate, he was stopped at Roissy airport following a banning order for the Schengen area issued by Germany.[17]

Secondly, intimidation has prevailed over the willingness to speak out in many instances. Thus, an investigation conducted among 1,000 teachers and researchers throughout the world specializing in the Middle East found that two-thirds of them admitted to self-censorship when referring to their area of expertise, the rate reaching 82 per cent in the United States and 70 per cent in the rest of the world when it came to the Israel–Palestine conflict specifically. In that regard, 52 per cent of the experts said they refrained from speaking on account of pressure from external advocacy groups, and 39 per cent because of possible disciplinary sanctions by their institution. In 70 per cent of cases, self-censorship intensified after 7 October and applied to criticism of Israel nine times more frequently than it did to criticism of the Palestinians.[18] The reluctance to speak out against the war is certainly understandable considering the repression against those defending the Palestinian cause, merely calling for a ceasefire, or even protecting free speech, with students deregistered from their institution, professors deprived of teaching and university presidents compelled to resign, in a context where pro-Israeli organizations, conservative politicians and wealthy donors exert considerable pressure on governing bodies in the United States.[19]

At Columbia University, where peaceful gatherings in solidarity with the Palestinians to demand a ceasefire in Gaza had been held since the start of the war, a chemical attack with toxic products was carried out on participants by two Israeli students who were former officers of the Israeli Occupation Forces, causing illnesses and hospitalizations, and a police raid on campus requested by the president resulted in more than 100 arrests.[20] At the University of California, Los Angeles, when a group of masked pro-Israeli militants assaulted students, including many Jews, who had set up camp to end the war, the police passively watched the attack for several hours, but the next day proceeded to clear the tents and arrest the pacifist demonstrators.[21] To justify law enforcement interventions on campus, the authorities and the media have often tried to discredit those protesting against the war by accusing them, often baselessly, of antisemitism and violence.[22] As demonstrations proliferated in late April in universities throughout the world, condemnation by national authorities and repression by the police were the rule, despite the generally inclusive character of the protests.[23] In most Western countries, then, the conditions for a respectful, open debate have not been met because of interference by the state, academic institutions and communal organizations. But it is in Israel that the repression against students, particularly Palestinians, has been harshest.[24]

There is no doubt that antisemitism exists in Western countries and, even if the equation of criticism of Israeli military intervention with discrimination against Jews renders measurement of it difficult, there is definitely a recrudescence with every Israeli military operation against the Palestinian Occupied Territories. In the United States, where Jewish students have recently complained about discrimination against them, and where the far right openly proclaims itself antisemitic, a survey of the general population indicates that a little over one-third of participants think that antisemitism is more prevalent than it was ten years ago. But, for half of them, the accusation of antisemitism serves to 'delegitimize political opponents' or to 'delegitimize critics of Israel'.[25] In France, where the Interior Ministry has noted that there were two-and-a-half times more complaints of antisemitic acts in 2023 than 2022, the increase occurring in the last three months of the year, the Israel–Palestine conflict is not solely responsible, for there are also older, more violent forms of antisemitism from the far right. However, contrary to what is often believed, the trend over the past decades has been towards greater tolerance.[26]

At the same time, there is no doubt that anti-Muslim and anti-Arab racism, and now anti-Palestinian violence, are also prevalent, although it receives less attention in the public sphere. In the United States, such complaints have nearly tripled since 7 October. A Palestinian child was stabbed, three youths of Palestinian origin were wounded by gunfire, Palestinian students and teachers have been subject to harassment, with their addresses published online, posters denouncing them displayed, and death threats issued.[27] In France, though it is conceded that they remain underestimated, Islamophobic acts also multiplied threefold in the fourth quarter of 2023.[28] The public authorities bear considerable responsibility here, as, far from soothing the tensions between groups, the way that they communalize them helps to fan them.

6

Without a doubt, what will haunt memories the longest, including perhaps in Israel itself, is how the inequality between lives has been paraded on the stage of Gaza, ignored by some and legitimized by others.[1] That this supreme injustice – one life being worth less than another – is widespread in our world is a reality evident in peacetime and wartime alike.[2] But there is hardly any previous instance in which the governments of Western countries so ostentatiously avert their eyes from it, to the extent of justifying it and silencing the voices that criticize it. Yet, of the conflicts that have occurred in the world in the twenty-first century, Israel's military interventions in Gaza have yielded the highest mortality differentials between civilian populations. According to data collected by the Israeli human rights organization B'Tselem, during Operation Cast Lead in 2008 the ratio of victims was 255 to 1 among civilians, while 318 children were killed in Gaza and none in Israel.[3] During Operation Protective Edge in 2014, according to figures from the independent commission of inquiry of the UN

Commission on Human Rights, the ratio was 244 to 1 among civilians, with 551 children being killed in Gaza and one in Israel.[4]

With the ongoing Operation Swords of Iron, the absolute number of Palestinian civilian victims will be several dozen times higher than during previous military interventions. After six months of war, 33,000 dead had already been identified in Gaza, to whom should be added around 10,000 more in the ruins of destroyed buildings. Estimates of the number of civilians among the victims are controversial, with the Israelis, in a manner deemed implausible by neutral sources, considering all males killed, regardless of age, to be members of Hamas.[5] If we consult more credible assessments and limit the calculation to the very conservative statistics of confirmed deaths, by 7 April, approximately 42 times more Palestinian than Israeli civilians had been killed.[6] As regards children, the ratio was already 420 to 1.[7] We can express this disparity differently by referring not to the absolute number of the deceased but to the mortality rate, so as to take account of the size of the relevant populations and thus more clearly convey the scale of the human losses for the societies concerned. Proceeding in this way, we find that, relative to their respective demography, among civilians, 185 times more Palestinians than Israelis have been killed. The mortality rate for children is 1,850 times higher among Palestinians. To measure the 7 October attack in Israel, it has been said that, as a proportion of the number of inhabitants of the two countries, it represented the equivalent of fifteen 9/11s in the United States.[8] Using the same comparison, we might add that total deaths in Gaza as of 7 April 2024 correspond to around seventeen hundred 9/11s. Relative to the population of the United States, the mortality registered in the Gaza Strip on 7 April would be, according to this very conservative estimation, five million casualties.

However, this macabre arithmetic only restores part of the reality, which it tends to render abstract. 'We Are Not Numbers' is the name of a project created for the children of Gaza in 2015 within the Euro-Mediterranean Human Rights Monitor organization. It aims to make the voice of Palestinians heard other than via statistics, for 'numbers are impersonal and often numbing'.[9] And these are mortality figures, as if Palestinian life could only be conceived in terms of its elimination. Yet, the deepest inequality is probably that of lives as they are lived. Throughout their existence, the experience of many Palestinians in their relationship with the State of Israel and its agents is one of exclusion, discrimination, belittlement, obstruction, destruction of their fields and houses, subjection to the violence and arbitrariness of authority. To use an evocative word, they are disposable, in two senses. They are at the state's disposal: they can be arrested at any time without a reason being given, imprisoned without charge and, where applicable, used as an exchange currency in negotiations – a practice validated by the Israeli Supreme Court.[10] And they can be disposed of: they can be killed or mutilated, generally with impunity because the Israeli government threatens the Palestinian Authority with reprisals should it bring any complaints before the International Criminal Court.[11] The public prosecutor of this institution has insisted that 'all attempts to impede, intimidate or improperly influence the officials of this court must cease immediately', adding that he 'would not hesitate to act' – an implicit reference to the threats made against his predecessor in the post when she launched an investigation into war crimes committed against the Palestinians. These threats to her and her family's safety came from the head of the Israeli secret service himself.[12]

One aspect of this existence has been analysed by the Israeli Palestinian criminologist, Nadera Shalhoub-Kevorkian, in a text on 'the occupation of the senses' in East Jerusalem, by which she meant the insinuation of power relations into the five senses of Palestinians through constant forms of 'micro-aggression' that 'colonize' bodies.[13] Thus, on various occasions, the police have sprayed the walls, streets and schools of the Arab quarters of the Holy City with putrid water whose odour was so revolting and persistent that the inhabitants could no longer go out, students had their education interrupted, and the contamination penetrated people's very bodies.[14] Moreover, for many years, Gaza has been overflown on a permanent basis by surveillance and attack drones, whose relentless buzzing is a constant noise pollution reminding the inhabitants of their status as a dominated population under threat.[15]

But most Western mainstream media virtually never refer to this reality. As the Palestinian professor of comparative literature Saree Makdisi writes, after 7 October they sought out Palestinian intellectuals to comment on Hamas's attack, but did not wish to hear from them about what had happened prior and what may happen subsequently.[16] It has often been said that the media silence on what residents of Gaza were living through was due to problems of access, given that the Israeli army was killing Palestinian journalists, prohibiting the presence of their foreign colleagues by allowing them to enter Gaza only when embedded, and sporadically interrupting Palestinians' communication with the external world. Despite these hindrances, however, reports were written there, testimonies were gathered, images were produced, which only social media and alternative outlets presented on their websites. But the truth is that it was predominantly a matter of editorial decisions, which some journalists said they deplored.

As analysed by Acrimed, mainstream French media, especially radio and television, have evinced 'selective compassion'.[17] They have reported the stories of freed Israeli hostages who complained of going hungry during their captivity in besieged Gaza, without mentioning the origin of the food shortages they suffered from. But they have not listened to the Palestinian civilians released from Israel's prisons and camps after being humiliated and tortured there. They have related the fears of Israeli schoolchildren near the border with Lebanon, obliged to take refuge in shelters when the sirens sound. But they have ignored the anguish of the Palestinian children of

Gaza, who have nowhere to seek refuge to escape the bombs that destroy whole neighbourhoods. They have interviewed Israeli surfers on the beach of Tel Aviv who explained that this activity calmed their anxiety in the wake of Iran's dispatch of drones and missiles. But they have often been content with one sentence to merely recall the number of dead Palestinians in Gaza, without speaking of the experience of women who can no longer breastfeed and children with nothing to eat.[18] Most broadcast media outlets have thus opted to humanize the Israelis, rather than the Palestinians. Thus, they reported at length on the 'success' of the military operation to free four Israelis held in a refugee camp on 8 June, and on the demonstrations of 'joy' when they were welcomed in Tel Aviv, mentioning only in passing the human cost of the rescue for Palestinians: 274 dead, including 64 children and 57 women, and 700 injured. On radio and television, the story was the 'liberation of the hostages'; in the independent media, the episode became known as the 'Nuseirat massacre'.[19]

There is nothing new about this; reports have long made the voice of the Israelis heard to the exclusion of that of the Palestinians. Meta has even removed messages written by Palestinians or supporters of their cause from Facebook and Instagram accounts, particularly when they reported human rights violations by the Israeli army; it has done so even where they were accompanied by peaceful statements.[20] Generally speaking, Palestinians' everyday resistance in the face of adversity and their demand to live in peace have been concealed from Western publics. There is an Arab concept often used to define their reaction to the ordeals of Israeli occupation and oppression: *sumud*, which signifies their tenacity, their perseverance, their ability to continue to live in a dignified way.[21] Since 7 October, the selective attention that has excluded them from the news has made it well-nigh impossible to know them other than as ruthless combatants or impersonal victims. A veil has been drawn over their despair at having been abandoned by the international community.

In a letter to their management, BBC reporters deplored this partiality in presenting the facts and, in particular, the unbalanced way a human dimension was conferred on the mourning of Israeli, but not Palestinian, families.[22] Elsewhere it was revealed that in a memorandum sent to *New York Times* journalists at the start of the war, the editors asked them to restrict employment of the words 'genocide' and 'ethnic cleansing', to avoid speaking of 'refugee camps' and 'occupied territories', and to mention 'Palestine' itself as infrequently as possible. They further indicated that unduly 'emotive' words such as 'slaughter', 'massacre' and 'carnage' should be replaced by factual descriptions – a recommendation that did not, however, apply to characterizing the 7 October attack.[23] Such instructions were no doubt commonplace in the mainstream US media for, according to a study of the language used to describe the victims on both sides in three of the country's main dailies, after three months of war the word 'horrific' appeared nine times more often to qualify Israeli deaths than Palestinian ones, the word 'massacre' thirty times more often, and the word 'slaughter' sixty times. As for 'children', victims who, dead or injured, numbered in the thousands, that word only figured on two occasions out of 1,100 headlines.[24] As early as November, more than 750 reporters from numerous US press organs criticized the one-sided coverage of the conflict.[25]

In general, at least during the initial months of the war – for some correction did gradually occur, making for a more balanced presentation of the facts – mainstream media, often contrary to some of their own journalists, adopted the language of Israeli government and military communications, known as *hasbara* and theorized as a weapon of war.[26] In fact, it was often in the independent and critical media – *Mediapart, Politis, L'Humanité, Blast* or *Orient XXI* in France; the *Boston Review*, the *Nation*, the *Intercept, Mondoweiss* in the US; the *London Review of Books* and *Middle East Eye* in the UK; +972 in Israel and Al Jazeera in the Arab world – that it was possible for people to be informed on the events in Gaza in a more neutral fashion, to hear Palestinian voices, to consult investigations free of Israeli communications, to access analyses independent of Western public authorities, and to read inquiries into facts which more established media organs often ended up adopting.

One index of this discrimination concerns the number of victims. Every time statistics for Palestinian deaths are given by journalists, they are accompanied by the formula 'according to the Gaza Health Ministry' or even 'according to the Hamas-run Health Ministry', whereas no equivalent phrase qualifies the data presented by the Israeli authorities.[27] This double standard is all the more remarkable for two reasons. First, the Israeli government exercises strict control over communications, making fact-checking especially difficult for journalists, notably regarding the true number of Hamas members killed or imprisoned. Second, during previous wars, figures from the Palestinian authorities, which have proved open to their external verification, have corresponded to those established by subsequent independent inquiries. 'I have no notion if Palestinians are telling the truth about how many people are killed', declared the US president on 25 October, adopting the argument of an Israeli army spokesman who claimed that the figures were always inflated, even though his own government employed them. The following day, the Gaza Health Ministry released a list of 6,747 victims with their name, age, sex and identity card number.[28] At the same time, a study published in one of the most prestigious international medical journals confirmed the data supplied by the Palestinian institution.[29] This querying of the number of dead is a double punishment for the victims of war. Their life has been taken; their death is denied.

Questioning the statistics is especially cynical given that mortality in Gaza is in fact heavily underestimated by the Palestinian administration. For one thing, it only counts bodies found and identified, leaving out those buried under ruins, whose corpses disappear in the rubble removed by Israeli bulldozers. For another, it does not record deaths from medical issues caused by malnutrition, dehydration or the absence of medicines, especially affecting the most vulnerable – the infants and the elderly. Only an epidemiological survey among the population after the event will be in a position to assess the excess mortality caused by the Israeli military operation. The study carried out by the Watson Institute on wars waged by the United States in the twenty-first century established that the number of indirect deaths linked to economic deterioration, food insecurity, infra-structure destruction, environmental contamination, the development of epidemics, and the devastation of the health system was four times greater than the number of direct deaths.[30] It is likely that on account not only of deaths attributable to the army, but also of the short- and medium-term impacts of famine, lack of hygiene, and absence of medical care, the war on Gaza will have produced more than 100,000 victims, a high proportion of them very young children, not to mention the enduring psychic trauma the survivors among them will suffer.[31]

But the Palestinians have been challenged over not only the quantification of the dead but also their catego-rization. To relativize the enormous disparity in the number of victims on either side, the equivalence between the meanings of these deaths has sometimes been called into question. It has been said that Israelis were killed as Jews, and thus denied their humanity, while Palestinians were killed accidentally, in the context of a military operation against an enemy.[32] This was, on one side, to reject Hamas's claim that its attack had been directed against an enemy that has deprived the Palestinian population of its land and its rights for more than half a century, which in no way excludes possible antisemitism; and, on the other, to ignore the statements by Israeli leaders and military officials that explicitly denied the humanity of the Palestinians, equating them with animals. The idea that the attack in southern Israel was crueller than the war in the Gaza Strip is probably linked to the fact that, in the former, the assailants and their victims are visible in the act of killing, whereas, in the latter, the bombardment and even the siege keep those who order them and those who execute the orders out of sight. Similarly, the cannon fire controlled by Israeli soldiers invisible in the turret of their tanks seems more impersonal and more disembodied than the automatic arms fire filmed by Palestinian combatants. The emotional distance felt by the spectator external to these scenes, whether in Israel or elsewhere in the world, is different. Yet it is not obvious that for the civilian victims and their loved ones there is any decisive difference between being killed in a kibbutz in Negev or on a street in Gaza – other, that is, than the difference between finding oneself on the side of the oppressor, who has been able to live like a free human being, or on the side of the oppressed, whose captive existence has unfolded under the menacing shadow of occupation.

After the national homage by the government to the French Israeli citizens who died on 7 October, a former

French president opined that no similar ceremony could be envisaged for the French Palestinian civilians who died during the war in Gaza, because a distinction had to be made between being killed 'as the defender of a way of life', in the first instance, and dying as a 'collateral victim', in the second.[33] That Palestinian mourning could be so minimized relative to Israeli mourning, despite the astounding numerical imbalance in the human losses in the two camps, reveals the iniquity of treatment even in death. As the US philosopher Judith Butler writes, some lives are grievable while others are not. Moreover, 'the differential distribution of grievability across populations has implications' for the conditions in which 'we feel politically consequential affective dispositions such as horror, guilt, righteous sadism, loss, and indifference', but also for the way in which it is possible, when it comes to lives not worth grieving over, to 'rationalize their death', since 'the loss of such populations is deemed necessary to protect the lives of the "living"'.[34] The distinction between these two levels of life is most blatantly and painfully displayed in the difference between the ability of Israeli families to bury their dead in a dignified and ritual fashion, notwithstanding the terrible reality of corpses sometimes burnt to ashes or dismembered by explosions, while for Palestinian families it is impossible to do likewise, either because the bodies are rotting under a mass of fallen rubble before, sometimes, being obliterated by mechanical diggers, or because there are too many corpses, which disappear into mass graves for want of space in cemeteries devastated by bombing, or even because the Israeli authorities refuse to return the remains of their loved ones to families, as has been shown by the French political scientist Stéphanie Latte Abdallah to be a long practice.[35]

It will have taken more than 30,000 official deaths, and probably more than 100,000 in reality, predominantly civilians and often children, for Western countries to begin to find the collective punishment sufficient; for their governments to envisage a ceasefire, though while continuing to send arms; and for their principal media to start correcting their partial presentation of events. But, as ever, the lost life of one Israeli civilian must be paid for by hundreds of Palestinian civilian lives, as if one was worth hundreds of times more than the other. 'The West has displayed sheer racism. It has implicitly asserted that a white life is worth more than an Arab life', argues the Palestinian journalist Lubna Masarwa.[36] Many of those who have demonstrated to demand a ceasefire were expressing their refusal of this inequality in lives.[37]

But political and media discourse has never reported the mobilization in such terms – that is, the Palestinians' right to life and their right to a good life. The situation has been described as a new 'campism', pitting a pro-Palestinian camp against a pro-Israeli one.[38] When people demanded a stop to the slaughter simply because you do not kill innocents, when they called for an end to the total siege simply because you do not starve human beings, when they condemned the devastation of

MORAL ABDICATION | 69

hospitals simply because you do not deprive the sick and wounded of medical care, when they criticized the destruction of schools and monuments simply because you do not strip a people of its culture and its history, it appeared that many commentators found it impossible to imagine a different camp: the camp of life.

Acquiescence to the war in Gaza and its tragic consequences has, for the foreseeable future, rendered any
invocation of human rights, humanitarian reason and
international law by those who have participated in this
moral abdication illegitimate and inoperative – even if it
must be acknowledged that their double standards in
many areas, including in their own countries, has long led
them to lose credibility on this score. The Western world
– or at least the majority of its rulers and institutions –
will have given virtually unconditional support not only
to the elimination of a large part of the Palestinian population, particularly the generation that represents its
future and hope, but also to the erasure of everything that
constitutes the soul of a people: schools, libraries, book-
shops, museums, cemeteries, religious buildings, historical monuments, cultural centres. It will have done so
while endeavouring to silence, through intimidation, stig-
matization and sanctions, researchers, intellectuals,
students, artists, activists, politicians and, more broadly,
citizens who refused to be associated with this abiding

crime, while, for its part, the Israeli army was silencing Palestinian academics, journalists, writers, poets, doctors and humanitarian workers by eliminating them.[1] Those in charge of French higher education and research institutions, although alerted by the members who were protesting against their silence, have not displayed the same solidarity with their Palestinian colleagues as they did with their colleagues in Ukraine, following its invasion by Russia, and in Israel, after the 7 October attack.[2] This was the case even as the Israeli army was destroying Gaza's universities, killing their presidents, their teachers, their students and their administrative and technical staff.[3] As the anthropologist Catherine Hass argued, the Israeli government wanted 'to create something irremediable in bodies and minds for everyone, to manufacture generations of illiterates in a society for which education and culture is important' – in short, to invert the title of the superb exhibition at the Paris Institut du Monde Arabe in 2023, 'to seek to ensure that Palestine no longer contributes anything to the world'.[4]

Doubtless, there is no need to search for precedents, which are probably all too obvious in the twentieth century, for this abandonment of the values that Western countries invoke as foundational. But we could certainly recall the global indignation at the destruction of the Buddhas of Bamiyan by the Taliban in 2001, or the bombing of the paediatric hospital in Mariupol by Russian troops in 2022 – episodes that prompted talk of 'barbarism' – to get a clearer sense of the imperviousness of the European and North American authorities to the destruction of Gaza's Great Mosque, dating from the thirteenth century, or the bombing of al-Shifa hospital, the largest in the region, in 2024. It is therefore necessary to try to comprehend what has made this moral abdication possible, by analysing, first, the reasoning behind the main argument used to justify Israel's unconditional right to defend itself, and second, the explanations that might account for the adhesion of so many governments to this argument and its deadly implications.

The 7 October attack convinced Israelis that the security they thought they had acquired was fragile, uncertain, threatened. Testimony and commentaries in the ensuing weeks revealed that this presumption, shared by many Jews throughout the world, went beyond dread in the face of the event. The crisis, they repeated, was existential in nature. Suddenly, so they said, the very survival of the State of Israel was in peril. To respond, as did the former head of the secret services Mossad, that a superarmed military and unwavering Western support made the risk of disappearance highly unlikely, did nothing to shake a conviction that fostered a sense of the need to eradicate the enemy.[5] This conviction was reinforced by the Israeli government, which found it useful in justifying an unlimited war where the death of tens of thousands of civilians would prove indispensable to liquidating several thousand militants. What justified the spectre of a danger to Israel's very existence was the intention expressed by Hamas in its 1988 Charter, conspiratorial and antisemitic in tone, which claimed the whole of historical Palestine for Muslims.[6] The Israeli argument rested, however, on a twofold sophistry: a projection that imagines in the other what one is doing oneself, and a self-realizing prophecy whereby one creates what one claims to counter.

Firstly, a revised version of Hamas's Charter was presented by its leader in 2017. Without clearly recognizing the State of Israel as had Fatah, it indicated the movement's advocation of a 'political solution' to the conflict, consisting in the creation of two states with the Palestinians having the territories defined by the borders of 1967, while it also recalled the historical claim to the whole of Palestine.[7] This political opening was thus not without its contradictions, bound up with compromises inside the movement. But it envisaged the start of negotiations on the basis of international law – something the Israeli government, which rejected UN resolutions, did not want. Before 7 October, Israel and its allies therefore preferred to consider the conciliatory posture of Hamas as insincere, in the same way they had done for Fatah's territorial accommodations a few decades earlier. After 7 October, they obviously felt confirmed in their distrust, while making no mention of their own rejection of any negotiation with Palestinians and non-implementation of the Oslo Accords.[8] In fact, since the 1950s the Israeli plan has been to conquer the whole of Palestine. Likud's 1977 Platform, eleven years prior to Hamas's first Charter, spelled it out: 'Between the Sea and the Jordan, there will only be Israeli sovereignty.'[9] As mentioned earlier, this claim was repeated by the Israeli prime minister at the UN General Assembly mere days before the 7 October attack.

In reality, this policy has been operative for more than five decades and, fifty years after the end of the Six-Day War, more than 100,000 hectares of land had already been seized, 600,000 settlers established in the Palestinian territories, 50,000 dwellings and structures demolished, and more than 5 million Palestinians deprived of freedom of movement in their own country.[10] The situation has grown worse since then. Following an intense campaign that permitted a 35 per cent increase in settler numbers between 2012 and 2022, it is estimated that 700,000 Israelis are illegally ensconced in 279 settlements in the West Bank – including fourteen in East Jerusalem, with 229,000 inhabitants – of which 147 are established in contravention of even Israeli law.[11] The first paradox of the supposed 'existential threat' is thus that, rejecting the change in Hamas's position, the Israeli government is able to accuse the Palestinians of imagining what it is itself in the process of doing.[12] As Rashid Khalidi has shown, the habitual denunciation of the formula 'from the river to the sea' as denying the existence of the Jewish state actually serves to conceal the fact that it is the latter which, by colonizing the West Bank and destroying Gaza, is on the point of fulfilling the dream of Eretz Israel.[13] To be precise, it should be pointed out that the first occurrence of that slogan dates back to the 1960s, when the PLO employed it with a view to a single state where Arabs, Jews and Christians could live in peace, in accordance with the wish expressed by Yasser Arafat before the UN General Assembly.[14] And to be optimistic, one might add that the phrase retains its meaning today if it is taken not in a spirit of conquest, as the Israeli government does, but in a spirit of reconciliation, as invoked, for example, by the Israeli–Palestinian human rights organization A Land for All, which seeks to envisage the possibility of two states in a peacefully shared territory.[15]

Secondly, in pursuing its project of the destruction of Gaza and its inhabitants, the Israeli government damages its country's image a little more every day and, consequently, also the image of its allies. The latter have begun to distance themselves from a country they continue to call a friend, but which they understand is dragging them into the abyss. Accused of genocide by a growing number of governments and experts throughout the world – an accusation implicitly validated by the ICJ – Israel has become an embarrassing geopolitical partner for Western leaders, who appreciate that they could, in their turn, be themselves charged with complicity in this crime – something that is already the case for some of them. The images of the systematic destruction of al-Shifa hospital, its maternity wing, its operating theatres, its emergency department whose more than one hundred beds were burnt, its neonatal intensive care department whose fourteen incubators were destroyed, its oxygen production unit which was wrecked – these revealed a determination to scuttle the Palestinian health system for good, as shown by a UN mission after the occupation of the site by the Israeli army which also caused the death, for want of treatment, of many sick and wounded people who had been hospitalized.[16] Information about the famine afflicting a large portion of the population, particularly infants, children and pregnant women; the refusal to allow the entry of most international aid; the carnage created by firing on people rushing to supply points; the bombing of the vehicles and facilities of humanitarian organizations – these have made it ever more difficult for the great powers to continue to avert their eyes from the Israeli government's project of crushing the Palestinian people, a project it has not ceased to publicize.[17]

Moreover, the decision made by the prosecutor of the International Criminal Court, on 20 May 2024, to apply for arrest warrants for the Israeli prime minister and his defence minister, as well as for three Hamas leaders, certainly adds to the discomfort of Western politicians.[18] The most ardent European defenders of the Israeli military operation, France and Germany in particular, have finally, prudently, called for a ceasefire. As for the United States, a State Department note warns that the Israelis 'are facing major, possibly generational damage to their reputation not just in the region but elsewhere in the world', which represents 'a major strategic error'.[19] Faced with the refusal by the Israeli prime minister to envisage a truce, in late March the US administration stopped vetoing a draft resolution of the UN Security Council demanding a halt to hostilities, while nevertheless continuing to send massive military aid to Israel.[20] The massacre of civilians and destruction of the territory, combined with hate speech against the Palestinian people, have thus internationally delegitimized not only the Israeli government, but more broadly Israeli society, a majority of which, including in the ranks of what was formerly called the left, supports the conduct of the war.[21]

On 7 June, *Haaretz*'s editorial headlined 'Brutalisation of Israel is well underway', denouncing the infiltration of the Israeli population, army, representatives and government by supremacist ideas, warned that if the country continued along this path, 'Israel's final fall will only be a matter of time.' It concluded: 'The countdown has begun.'[22] On 3 July, after the release of the director of al-Shifa hospital, who had been detained without charge for seven months, a famous Israeli columnist wrote, also in *Haaretz*, that 'anyone who wants to learn what's happened to Israelis' must observe how society has reacted to this event. Stressing that the image of 'an innocent hostage' just freed from jail 'hugging his mother and crying should have had an emotional effect on any human being', he said that what he witnessed instead was a 'hysterical campaign of panic, incrimination, hatred, dehumanisation, lust for vengeance, thirst for blood' within the political world, in the media and among the public.[23] Even if Western journalists almost systematically conceal these facts, out of sympathy for the Israeli government or to avoid being accused of antisemitism, the news eventually filter through other channels. Polls show that a favourable image of Israel declined by more than 18 per cent on average in the forty-three largest countries on the planet between September and December 2023.[24] Thus, the Jewish state and its champions are symbolically precipitating the existential threat they insist they wish to avert.[25]

So why have most Western governments supported not only Israel's right to defend itself, but also its plan to obliterate Gaza? Why did they not react when the Israeli president asserted that a 'whole nation' was responsible, thus foreshadowing the mass murder to come? Why, on the eve of the commemoration of the thirtieth anniversary of the genocide of the Tutsis, did the French president admit that France along with its Western and African allies 'could have stopped it' but 'lacked the will' to do so, without making the connection with the fact that, for six months, he had found himself in a position to intervene, along with his Western and possibly Arab allies, in an effort to prevent what the highest international court regarded as a plausible risk of genocide in Gaza, but lacked the will to do so – something that three decades hence his successor may admit?[26] As far as the European states are concerned, it is, in Mona Chollet's words, a question of 'absolving themselves of their guilt in the Shoah', and of delegating to Israel the 'role of guardian of their interests in the Middle East'.[27] The two elements are more closely connected than is generally realized.

Over and above the profound emotion aroused by the suddenness and violence of Hamas's attack, frequently invoked is what in 2008 the former German chancellor called Israel's security as 'raison d'état'.[28] What is true of her country when it comes to the history of the genocide of European Jews applies, albeit to a lesser degree, to others, including France, who collaborated with the Nazis. Without challenging the sincerity of many of those who today, especially in Germany, are convinced that Israel must be supported whatever the cost, it is necessary to subject this noble desire for redemption to a critical examination of what also pertains to realpolitik.

In the aftermath of the Second World War, Germany moved in that direction. The extensive financial reparations initiated then, and the unconditional support given to the young State of Israel, partook not only of ethical compunction but also of 'strategic philosemitism'.[29] Chancellor Konrad Adenauer justified it by his desire to restore Germany's 'international standing' and by his concern to make Israel the 'fortress of the West' – at the very time he was abandoning the policy of de-Nazification and endeavouring to protect certain former dignitaries of the Third Reich. The British Israeli architect Eyal Weizman notes the disturbing paradox, and apparent amnesia about this historical ambiguity, of German political officials accusing the children or grandchildren of survivors of the destruction of the Jews in Europe of antisemitism, at the same time as they endorse a plan for the destruction of the Palestinians in Gaza.[30]

The historical reasons are thus compounded by geopolitical stakes, where the interests of the Europeans and North Americans converge with those of several Middle Eastern countries, particularly Saudi Arabia, the United Arab Emirates and the Kingdom of Bahrain, as well as, for a long time, Egypt and Jordan. They are working together to create both a major regional market, which presupposes normalizing relations with Israel, and a common front against Iran and its allies, as shown with the military cooperation between Western and Arab armies during the drone and missile attack launched by the mullahs in response to Israel's airstrike on the Iranian consulate in Damascus, which had killed thirteen people, including two generals.[31] In this configuration, which has significant economic and military implications for all parties, strengthening the partnerships sealed by the Abraham Accords implies the repudiation of the Palestinian problem, rather than its resolution. The situation prior to 7 October was therefore auspicious, since there was no longer any interest in the Palestinians and their potential sovereignty, allowing Israel to enjoy carte blanche for the extension of its settlements, including in Jerusalem, and suffocating the populations of Gaza and the West Bank. In fact, the geopolitical issues tend to be highlighted by the United States in preference to the historical reasons, which might reveal similarities between the genesis of their own country and that of the State of Israel.[32] The US government is indeed predominantly concerned with power relations, in the context of a reshaping of international alliances, a resurgence of imperialisms, and a revived Atlanticism.

A significant, but often neglected aspect of support for Israel is the contribution to the global arms industry and, more broadly, to the war economy. It was France under the Fourth Republic that enabled Israel to acquire nuclear weapons – a programme officially repealed by

General de Gaulle in 1960, but which continued unofficially until 1968.[33] Today, however, the aid given by the United States is by far the largest, greatly exceeding all its other grants to foreign countries. Since 1946 it has amounted to $310 billion. In recent years it stood at $3.3 million per annum, 99.7 per cent of it destined for the military sector, plus $500 million to strengthen the protective dome against aerial attack. On average, this contribution represents 71 per cent of the international aid received by Israel and 15 per cent of its defence budget.[34] On 19 April 2024, an additional $17 billion of military aid was approved by Congress, over and above the $14 billion already allocated some months earlier. Before submitting this draft legislation, the US president noted that his country would not supply military aid to foreign governments guilty of flagrant human rights violations, in accordance with the Leahy Law that established this rule, which is thus supposed to have been respected by Israel over recent decades and even, despite the ICJ order, since 7 October.[35] As with all grants made by the United States for defence purposes, the recipients are required to spend the sums allocated on purchasing US matériel and services, with some exceptions being authorised in the case of Israel. This means that the aid is, in fact, a subsidy to the US military-industrial complex. Just like the war in Ukraine, then, the war in Gaza represents a major resource for firms in this sector, but also for the expertise developed by the Pentagon in the global arms race. More broadly, in addition to the financial returns they procure for the United States, as for Germany, France, Italy and Britain, sales of military matériel and services to Israel have the advantage of putting them to the test of actual combat situations.

The Israeli prime minister knows how to utilize these multiple dimensions of Western support. In addition to invoking the existential threat to the State of Israel, he does not fail to recall that he is the representative and defender of the 'civilized world' in the region.[36] Meanwhile, it is likely that in the current resurgence of authoritarianism and nationalism, including the spectacular progress of far-right parties in much of Europe – several of which are now in government – tolerance or even sympathy for this ally is related to his exercise of power, which exalts those tendencies. This would explain the close affinity between the antisemitic Hungarian prime minister and his supremacist Israeli colleague.

In the case of the United States, there is a more trivial reason for the Democratic administration's support for Israeli policy. It is bound up with the role of the American Israel Public Affairs Committee (AIPAC), the principal external financier of Democratic primaries, which has vowed to spend $100 million to eject candidates who support a cease-fire. It also made a substantial donation to the campaign expenses of the Republican speaker of the House of Representatives, after he secured approval of the draft legislation donating $14 billion of military aid to Israel.[37]

Alongside these various logics – historical, geopolitical, economic, military and electoral – whose configurations vary with national contexts, one element is common to Western countries. It is ideological. It manifests itself in hostility towards Muslims and racism against Arab populations. Both form part of a colonial heritage, especially for the French and British empires, and even of a pre-colonial heritage, for what Maxime Rodinson dubbed the 'Christian West'.[38] But this rejection assumed a different meaning after 11 September 2001. Islam became associated with terrorism, Muslims with a danger to the security of Western countries, and Arab populations with a threat to European identity. There has been a proliferation of xenophobic discourse specifically aimed at all three, with the theme of the 'Great Replacement' being disseminated just like once the Judeo-Masonic conspiracy, the tightening of border restrictions such as the so-called Muslim ban in the United States, the prohibition of religious signs linked to Islam in France, the rise of Islamophobia documented in a recent report in Germany, and, most strikingly, the withdrawal of Belgian nationality from the children of Palestinian parents born in Belgium.[39] Such discrimination against Muslims is exposed by the selectivity of European immigration policies, evident in the unequal treatment of Ukrainian exiles fleeing the Russian invasion, who were generously welcomed, and Afghan exiles fleeing Taliban repression, who were brutalized at the Greek, Croatian and Hungarian borders.[40] But animosity towards Muslims also fosters sympathy for the Israeli government and support for its repression of the Palestinian population elsewhere in the world, particularly in India, where the prime minister pursuing an openly Islamophobic policy at home maintains a warm relationship with his Israeli counterpart that has been characterized as a 'bromance' in the media.[41]

The expression 'Muslims are the new Jews' has become common in recent social science literature, positing the idea that Europe's historical antisemitism has today been replaced by Islamophobia.[42] It is probably not so much an interconnected phenomenon as two processes obeying distinct logics and proceeding at different speeds. However, mistrust and antipathy, along with discrimination on the part of citizens and governments alike, currently affect Muslims significantly more than Jews. This is notably the case in France, where according to a poll conducted in 2021, people who considered that anti-Muslim racism is widespread were nearly twice the number of those who made the same observation for antisemitism; while those stating they would be uncomfortable with Muslim neighbours were four times more numerous than those expressing the same discomfort if their neighbours were Jewish.[43] A remarkable phenomenon in the evolution of these two forms of ethnoreligious rejection is the rapprochement lately effected between the far right, whose foundational antisemitism has been superseded by an Islamophobic obsession, and a section of French Jewry. This involves some of their most authoritative representatives, who openly display their inclination towards the National Rally, as well as part of the

Jewish electorate in France or settled in Israel, who vote massively for the Reconquest party.[44] A similar rapprochement is underway in Germany.

In this context, where the Western imaginary readily associates Palestinians with a triple stigma – as Arabs, as Muslims, and as represented by political parties formerly or currently characterized as terrorist – it comes as no surprise that, before 7 October, the Palestinian cause could hardly make itself heard and that, after that date, the very survival of the Palestinian people could no longer be defended. Yet, as the Israeli legal scholar Chaim Gans writes: 'It is not the Palestinians who have persecuted the Jews continuously throughout the second millennium in Europe, nor was it in their society that the civic emancipation of the Jews tragically failed during the nineteenth and twentieth centuries.' So, he asks: 'Without their explicit consent to paying the price, how can imposing that price be justified?'[45] This is perhaps the ultimate key to interpreting the consent of Western countries to the obliteration of Gaza: atonement by proxy for their participation in the genocide of European Jews, even if it means allowing a second Nakba to be inflicted on a population whose sacrifice the world had already accepted.

8

The present crisis is one of the deepest experienced since the time, nearly eight decades ago, when people first proclaimed: 'Never again.' But here, the word 'crisis' does not refer to the situation in Gaza. For it is the wrong descriptor for a military operation aiming to destroy a people as such, its memory, its material culture, the possibility of a livable life – whether or not jurists and historians may one day decide to characterize it as 'genocide', following symbolic power struggles in which Western governments will pit all their weight against it. Even to speak of a 'humanitarian crisis' – however legitimate it is to assert the right to survival of men, women and children reduced to extreme conditions, and to demand they accede to the minimum assistance they have been denied – is to avoid naming things for what they are, by designating the effects without stating the cause; and to justify a demand for 'humanitarian corridors and pauses' while permitting the continued bombardment of civilians in apparent respect for international law.[1]

No, the crisis at stake concerns the world that has watched with indifference the progressive erasure of the Palestinian Occupied Territories for more than half a century, and has allowed the abrupt disappearance within a few months of part of what defines them. In the case of most European and North American countries as well as various others, this has meant not mere passivity but unconditional political and military support for Israel. This alliance has elicited indignation from those who, while condemning the bloody acts that triggered it, refused to condone the massacre being perpetrated, and who have been stigmatized and repressed for it.

Language is damaged when demands to stop killing civilians are 'antisemitic', when an army that dehumanizes its enemies is 'moral', when an enterprise of obliteration is a 'riposte', when a military operation openly conducted against Palestinian civilians is the 'Israel–Hamas war'. Thinking is suffocated when debates are prevented, lectures banned and exhibitions cancelled, when the police enter institutions of higher education and prosecutors are imposed to ensure orthodoxy. An oppressive atmosphere of suspicion and accusation has endangered freedom of speech. An attempt to misuse words and invert values has put political understanding and moral discernment to the test. In a reflection on the language of genocide, entitled 'Who are the assassins of memory?', the French historian Pierre Vidal-Naquet analysed the way in which the use of a 'coded language' had served, at different moments, discursive strategies to rewrite history, quoting Thucydides on the

Peloponnesian War: 'Even the usual meaning of words in relation to acts was changed in the justifications given for them.'[2] These falsifications justify that social scientists, with humility but determination, make their truth heard, however fragile it may be.[3]

In particular, they can explore the past in search of examples capable of cutting through the opacity of the present to imagine the possibility of a future. At a time when the spirit of vengeance predominates on the Israeli side, when war is an end in itself, when any peaceful solution is rejected, when the very existence of the Palestinian people is denied, such a prospect seems inconceivable. And yet, it is enough to think of South Africa in the final years of apartheid. The parallel between the two historical situations may find some justification in two facts. The country which has initiated the proceedings against the State of Israel for its violations of the Convention on the Prevention and Punishment of the Crime of Genocide is South Africa. The ruling of the ICJ declaring the occupation of the Palestinian Territories by Israel unlawful refers explicitly to situations of segregation and apartheid.[4]

Certainly, in 1994, South Africa had not experienced slaughter and destruction on a par with those in Gaza. But it was on the brink of civil war, attacks had been carried out, the repression of opponents was ferocious, and racial supremacism had reached levels that have rarely been equalled. Nevertheless, the transition to a democratic regime was achieved. Treating 'South Africa as a model', Barbara Cassin has identified the three conditions of success that had to come together to make the transition from war to reconciliation, and thereby deal with hatred: 'a policy of remembrance, a policy of justice, and a policy of speech'.[5] None of them is unambiguous – remembrance between amnesia and anamnesis, justice between amnesty and reparation, speech between performative discourse and linguistic exhaustion – as was demonstrated by the divisions and resentment that emerged a little later.[6] But the worst was avoided, and cohabitation between the erstwhile oppressor and oppressed was made possible.

For negotiations to begin between the White government and the Black majority, three historical factors were combined: the existence of internal resistance mobilizations of various stripes, from the Black Consciousness Movement and the Mass Democratic Movement to trade unions and Christian churches, whose struggles converged; the proliferation of external forms of pressure, notably boycott, disinvestment and sanctions campaigns by some Western countries, including the United States, and even an arms sales embargo decided at the UN, which undermined the regime; finally, the presence of a charismatic, visionary leader, Nelson Mandela, and a pragmatic president, F. W. de Klerk.

The gulf between the historical South African situation and the current Israeli situation is unquestionably abyssal.[7] Firstly, the left sympathetic to the Palestinian cause in Israel is crushed and inaudible, and where there is strong opposition to the government it essentially concerns internal issues, whereas surveys show that adherence to the destruction of Gaza and its population is very widespread. Secondly, Western countries wholeheartedly support the Israeli government and several of them even criminalize boycott, disinvestment and sanctions campaigns, something that has earned France the condemnation of the European Court of Human Rights for illegal repression. Thirdly, and finally, the highly popular leader Marwan Barghouti, cast by many as a possible negotiator and future president of the Palestinian Authority, has been sentenced to five life terms, while no Israeli politician seems ready to entertain the possibility of talks. Yet voices have made themselves heard on both sides for a just and lasting peace: what is to come is therefore not yet written.

'In the short run history may be made by the victors,' wrote Reinhart Koselleck, 'but in the long run gains in historical understanding have come from the vanquished.'[8] Since 7 October, victors' history is what is being written, by Israel on the ground and by Western countries through the construction of a narrative that brooks no dissent. But a different history will probably be written one day. It will place in perspective the decades of oppression and resistance, dispossession and hope, peaceful struggles and violent revolts, and a culture that has survived beyond destructive passion. A voice will be restored to the Palestinians and with it a language will be reborn. Words will find their true meaning again. A war of annihilation will no longer be called a 'riposte'. An army practising torture on civilians will no longer be regarded as 'moral'. 'Antisemitism' will no longer be used to describe a call for justice and dignity. People will no longer dare to claim that some people's lives are worth less than others' and that the death of the former is not as grievable as that of the latter. It will be understood that the dehumanization of the enemy entails the loss of humanity of those who articulate it. Like Walter Benjamin's angel, 'his face turned toward the past' where he sees a 'catastrophe which keeps piling wreckage upon wreckage', while others perceive only 'a chain of events', we will realize the scale of the strange defeat experienced by the Western world.[9]

This other history will no longer be inspired by lies and hatred, but by truth and hope, as dreamed of by the Palestinian poet Refaat Alareer, professor at the Islamic University of Gaza, shortly before dying on 7 December 2023 in a targeted bombing attack on the flat where he had taken refuge with his sister, who was likewise killed, as was his brother and four of his nephews and nieces:[10]

> If I must die,
> you must live
> to tell my story
> to sell my things
> to buy a piece of cloth
> and some strings
> (make it white with a long tail)
> so that a child, somewhere in Gaza
> while looking heaven in the eye

awaiting his dad who left in a blaze –
and bid no one farewell
not even to his flesh
not even to himself –
sees the kite, my kite you made, flying up
above
and thinks for a moment an angel is there
bringing back love
If I must die
let it bring hope
let it be a tale[11]

Coda

In the days following Hamas's attack, I wrote to my Israeli friends and colleagues, and to those who had family in Israel, to express my sympathy and find out whether any of their relatives were among the victims. Fortunately, such was not the case, but I realized what a profound trauma they had experienced. After the bombing and siege of Gaza had begun, I also wrote to my Palestinian friends and colleagues, whether resident in Palestine or not, to show my solidarity and inquire about their situation and that of their family. This enabled me to register the degree of desolation and isolation they were experiencing in the face of such massive bereavement. The present essay is an attempt to analyse what made it impossible for a majority of the leaders, and many among the elites, in Western countries, to grasp the meaning of these two series of events and recognize the ethical responsibility they entailed.

It manifests the will to leave a trace – an archive – of the months during which I reflected and worried, like so many others, about the drama being played out on two stages: one local, in Palestine; the other global, in the West. At a time when the space for debate had been significantly reduced by intimidation, accusations and calumny of which I had my share, and threats, sanctions and convictions from which numerous others suffered, it seemed more necessary than ever to resist the twofold scourge of censorship and self-censorship, by making a modest contribution to freedom of critical expression. This contribution bears on the moral questions and political issues in contemporary societies at the heart of my lectures at the Collège de France, of which the recent events are a tragic textbook case.

First in France, and then in the United States, my thinking was nourished not only by reading and listening to the news about ongoing events and the reactions they elicited, but also by meetings and conversations with colleagues from various countries holding diametrically opposed views on the situation in the Middle East. I spoke with a German representative from the governing party, a former Palestinian prime minister, Israeli researchers and French journalists, and with legal scholars, political scientists, sociologists and anthropologists from different academic domains. In the months and years to come, countless works will no doubt enrich our knowledge and understanding of what happened on 7 October and its aftermath and how European and North American countries responded to it. The sole ambition of the present text is to attest to the existence of a refusal, shared by many, of consent to the obliteration of Gaza.

In this respect, I want to pay homage to the courage of those, notably students, Jewish and non-Jewish, in the United States, France and elsewhere in the world who, rejecting any form of antisemitism, have dared to stand up to defend the rights of Palestinians – their right to life and to a life of dignity, their right to a just and lasting peace – and have done so despite denunciation from their institutions, attacks from governments, media disinformation, police repression and judicial punishment. In retrospect, they will emerge as right-eous, affirming, despite the threats hanging over them, the principles of humanity.

I express my thanks to the hundreds of people, many of them colleagues, who in private or in public have shown me support when I was the target of malevolent attacks. I am indebted to Dirk Moses and Tobias Haberkorn for their invitation to write, in the *Journal of Genocide Research* and the *Berlin Review* respectively, articles that allowed me to broach some of the questions of the present essay, which benefited from the grant awarded by the Nomis Foundation. I am grateful to Bruno Auerbach for his warm support for this project at La Découverte, to Sebastian Budgen for his immediate interest in the book at Verso, to Timothy Mitchell for his role as gracious ambas-sador, to Gregory Elliott for his fine translation and to Lorna Scott Fox, Mark Martin and Nick Walther for their meticulous editing. I am thankful to Yazid Ben Hounet, Yasmine Bouagga, Sonja Brentjes, Michel Gros, Ghassan Hage, Abdelalli Hajjat, Catherine Hass, Stefan-Ludwig Hoffman, Justine Lacroix, Lee Mordechai, Ron Naiweld,

Deborah Poritz, Joan Scott, Edna Widgerson, and many others, including Camille, Baptiste and Thomas Fassin, with whom I have had exchanges, sometimes brief, sometimes sustained, that have enchanced my analysis. I owe profound gratitude to Fadi Bardawil, Wendy Brown, Darryl Li, Nadia Marzouki and an anonymous reader for Verso, who all made useful observations on initial versions of the manuscript, the writing of which was patiently accompanied by Anne-Claire Defossez with her judicious comments.

Obviously, as is customary to state, but in this instance unquestionably important to repeat, this text is solely my responsibility.

Princeton, 7 April 2024–Paris, 7 May 2024

Notes

Preface

1 Brian Klug, 'George Orwell, Gaza, and "the debasement of language"', *Contending Modernities*, 15 December 2023.
2 Talal Asad, 'Reflections on the Israeli-Palestinian conflict', *Humanity*, 21 March 2024.
3 This famous line comes from an aphorism attributed to Hillel the Elder, a luminary of the rabbinic tradition and founder of a religious school in the late first century BCE: 'If I am not for myself, who will be? If I am only for myself, what am I? If not now, when?' Primo Levi borrowed this question for the title of one of his novels: *Se non ora, quando?* IfNotNow is also the name of a Jewish movement fighting for the equality of Palestinians and Israelis.

Chapter 1

1 Official data published by the Israeli administration in December 2023: france24.com/en.live-news/20231215.
2 Julia Frankel and Alon Bernstein, 'Israeli army probing death of 12 hostages in Kibbutz Be'eri house shelled on orders of senior officer', *Haaretz*, 6 February 2024.

3 B'Tselem, 'Human beings are not bargaining chips – release the captives now', 23 October 2023.

4 Nicolas Rouger, 'Crimes du Hamas: qu'y a-t-il dans la vidéo de 48 minutes d'horreur que montre Tsahal à la presse étrangère', *Libération*, 2 November 2023.

5 Ellen Ioannes, 'What the UN report on October 7 sexual violence does – and doesn't – say', *Vox*, 7 March 2024.

6 Nir Hasson and Liza Rozovsky, 'Hamas committed documented atrocities. But a few false stories feed the deniers', *Haaretz*, 4 December 2023.

7 Adam Rasgon and Natan Odenheimer, 'Israeli soldier's video undercuts medic's account of sexual assault', *New York Times*, 25 March 2024.

8 The Short String, 'Family of key case in *New York Times* October 7 sexual violence report renounces story, says reporters manipulated them', *Mondoweiss*, 3 January 2024.

9 Special Representative of the Secretary General on Sexual Violence in Conflict, 'Mission Report, 29 January–14 February 2024', 4 March 2024.

10 Mary Tufah, 'Atrocity propaganda vs. testimony of atrocity', *Mondoweiss*, 31 March 2024.

11 Jeet Heer, 'Why Netanyahu bolstered Hamas', *Nation*, 11 December 2023.

12 Noa Shpigel, 'Israeli Finance minister sparks outrage after saying returning Gaza hostages "not most important thing"', *Haaretz*, 20 February 2024.

13 According to this survey, one-third of Jewish Israelis declared themselves in favour of a total annexation of the Occupied Territories and of the creation of an Israeli state encompassing the whole of Palestine. International MA Program in Conflict Resolution and Mediation, 'Findings – The Peace index – November 2023', social-sciences.tau.ac.il.

14 Testimony reported on CNN: twitter.com/AGvaryahu/.

15 Julien Sauvaget, 'Hommage aux victimes du Hamas: Macron dénonce "le plus grand massacre antisémite de notre siècle"', *France 24*, 7 February 2024.

16 Christophe Ayad, 'Le conflit Israël-Hamas s'invite dans les tribunaux français', *Le Monde*, 2 March 2024. A seventy-three-year-old elected French municipal official of Tunisian origin was summoned to a criminal court for 'apologizing for terrorism' after simply posting without comment on a Facebook group a quote from the former Tunisian minister of Foreign Affairs, which described the 7 October attack as an 'act of resistance'. He was also expelled from the Socialist Party.

17 Leila Seurat, 'À Gaza comme en Cisjordanie, les Palestiniens sont unanimes dans leur soutien au Hamas', *Le Monde*, 29 October 2023, and *The Foreign Policy of Hamas: Ideology, Decision-Making, and Political Supremacy*, London, I.B. Tauris, 2019.

18 Adam Shatz, 'Vengeful pathologies', *London Review of Books*, 45 (21), 2 November 2023.

19 Abdaljawad Omar, 'Hopeful pathologies in the war for Palestine', *Mondoweiss*, 8 November 2023.

20 Tareq Baconi, *Hamas Contained: The Rise and Pacification of Palestinian Resistance*, Stanford, Stanford University Press, 2018, p. 17.

21 George Orwell, *Nineteen Eighty-Four*, London, Secker and Warburg, 1949.

22 Balazs Berkovits, 'The October 7 pogrom as a non-event on the Western left', *Revue K*, 25 January 2024.

23 See, for instance, 'Israel at war', *Haaretz*, 5 January 2024.

24 Rashid Khalidi, *The Hundred Years' War on Palestine: A History of Settler Colonialism and Resistance 1917–2017*, New York, Picador, 2020.

25 Charles de Gaulle, Press conference, 27 November 1967, *INA*, fresques.ina.fr/de-gaulle/fiche-media.

26 António Guterres, 'Secretary General's remarks to the

Security Council – on the Middle East', United Nations, 24 October 2023, un.org/sg/en.

27 Hala Alyan, 'The Palestine double standard', *New York Times*, 25 October 2023.

28 Mitch Ginzburg, 'When Moshe Dayan delivered the defining speech on Zionism', *Times of Israel*, 28 April 2016.

29 Eyal Weizman, 'Exchange rate', *London Review of Books*, 45 (21), 2 November 2023.

30 Alain Frachon, 'Dans la gamme du terrorisme de masse, le Hamas a déchaîné contre une population civile une barbarie singulière', *Le Monde*, 12 October 2023. In his interview on CNN, 12 November 2023, Benjamin Netanyahu declares: 'It's your war too. It's the battle of civilization against barbarism', cnn.com.

31 Alon Pinkas, 'Netanyahu is on brand: no responsibility, no accountability, no remorse', *Haaretz*, 13 October 2023.

32 Hagar Shezaf, '2022 saw highest number of Palestinians killed in West Bank by Israeli forces since Second Intifada', *Haaretz*, 4 January 2023.

33 The illegal barrier that was to encircle the village was finally abandoned by the Israeli government, which decided to build it on the Green Line separating the Jewish State and the Occupied Territories. The 2009 film *Budrus*, directed by Julia Bacha, received several awards.

34 United Nations, *Two Years On: People Injured and Traumatized during the 'Great March of Return' are still Struggling*, 6 April 2020. During the 2018 and 2019 protests, while incendiary kites were used by some Palestinians, live ammunition systematically fired by Israelis targeted the lower limbs, particularly the knees, causing severe injuries very difficult to repair. One sniper boasted to the press that he had wounded forty-two Palestinians in one day.

35 Unicef, *The Gaza Strip: The Humanitarian Impact of Fifteen Years of Blockade*, June 2022.

36 Human Rights Council, *Report of the Special Rapporteur on the Situation of Human Rights in the Palestinian Territories Occupied since 2007*, United Nations, 15 June – 3 July 2020.

37 Nicolas Sarkozy, interview, *France 3*, 26 September 2005, vie-publique.fr/discours.

38 Judith Levine, 'There was no cover-up of Hamas's sexual violence on October 7', *Intercept*, 24 December 2023. Thus, despite having condemned on 13 October 2023 'the attacks against civilians in Israel and the Palestinian Territories' and declaring itself 'deeply alarmed by the catastrophic impact on women and girls', the organization UN Women was targeted by a hostile campaign under the slogan '#Metoo unless you're a Jew'.

Chapter 2

1 Henry Laurens, 'Terrorisme, l'impossible éradication de l'"ennemi"', *Orient XXI*, 2 July 2015. Professor at the Collège de France, Henry Laurens is the author of a five-volume history of *La Question de Palestine*.

2 Mathias Delori, 'The "global war on terror" and the fetishism of lesser intentionality', *Political Anthropological Research on International Social Sciences*, 21 June 2022.

3 Alexis Coskun, 'Les listes d'organisations terroristes, un instrument juridique éminemment politique', *Recherches internationales*, 101, 2014: 149–60. Seventeen of the twenty-one organizations deemed terrorist by the European Union in 2024 come from Muslim countries: eur-lex.europa.eu/.

4 Michel Warschawski, 'We have gone beyond war crimes in Gaza', Verso Blog, 6 November 2023.

5 The wording of Resolution 67/19, adopted by the UN General Assembly on 29 November 2012, echoed the terms

of several previous resolutions. Nine months after the start of the war in Gaza, four new European countries had recognized the State of Palestine: Spain, Ireland, Norway and Slovenia. On 28 May 2024, the French president nevertheless rejected what he described as 'an emotional recognition', in defiance of international law and in contradiction with France's vote at the UN in favour of recommending the admission of Palestine as a 'state in its own right': Marc Daou, 'Reconnaissance de l'État palestinien: c'est "le bon moment" pour la France', *France 24*, 30 May 2024.

6 Ishaan Tharoor, 'Welcome to the new, "new" Middle East', *Washington Post*, 16 October 2023.

7 Lazar Berman, 'France slams Smotrich's "infuriating" claim that Palestinian nation doesn't exist', *Times of Israel*, 21 March 2023.

8 As soon as late October 2023, the US president emphasized the 'need for a Palestinian state': Yasmeen Abutaleb, 'Biden, shifting tone, stresses need for Palestinian state', *Washington Post*, 25 October 2023. But behind the scenes, the White House was opposed to this move, as shown by diplomatic telegrams urging members of the UN Security Council to vote against the text proposing the recognition of the State of Palestine as a UN full member: Ken Klippenstein and Daniel Boguslaw, 'Leaked cables show White House opposes Palestinian statehood', *Intercept*, 17 April 2024.

9 Lev Luis Grinberg, 'Resistance, politics and violence: The catch of the Palestinian struggle', *Current Sociology*, 6 (2): 206–25.

10 'After 75 years of relentless occupation and suffering, and after failing all initiatives for liberation and return to our people, and also after the disastrous so-called peace process, what did the world expect the Palestinian people to do in response' to the abandonment of the international

community and the complicity of the superpowers in the face of the blockade of Gaza, the colonization of the West Bank, the millions of refugees in camps, the refusal of the creation of a Palestinian state? ask Hamas leaders in a document entitled *Our Narrative . . . Operation Al-Aqsa Flood*: palestinechronicle.com.

11 Opinion poll conducted by the Palestinian Center for Policy and Survey Research between 22 November and 2 December 2023. Of the 1,231 individuals included in the survey, 82 per cent in the West Bank and 57 per cent in Gaza stated that they supported Hamas's military operation: pcpsr.org/en/node/963.

Chapter 3

1 International Court of Justice, *The Republic of South Africa institutes proceedings against the State of Israel and requests the Court to indicate provisional measures*, 29 December 2023, icj-cij.org/index.

2 OpinioJuris, 'Public statement: Scholars warn of potential genocide in Gaza', twailr.com.

3 Office of the High Commissioner for Human Rights, 'Gaza: UN experts decry bombing of hospitals and schools as crimes against humanity, call for prevention of Genocide', United Nations: ohchr.org/en/press-releases.

4 'Defense for Children – Palestine v. Biden', uscourts.gov.

5 International Federation for Human Rights, 'The unfolding genocide against the Palestinians must stop immediately', fidh.org.

6 For example, the former Israeli ambassador Élie Barnavi stated that 'with the power differential that exists on the ground, if we had wanted to commit a genocide, it would not be 32,000 Palestinian civilians that would be deplored, but 200,000', *Mediapart*, 4 April 2024. In fact, the number of

victims does not define genocide (however, some projections suggest that the number of Palestinian lives lost might be close to 200,000 when the final death count will be done).

7 Office of the High Commissioner for Human Rights, *Convention on the Prevention and Punishment of the Crime of Genocide*, United Nations, 9 December 1948.

8 Omer Bartov, 'What I believe as a historian of genocide', *New York Times,* 10 November 2023.

9 United Nations, 'Press Conference by Secretary-General António Guterres', 22 December 2023, press.un.org.

10 All data and sources can be found in the document Republic of South Africa, 'Application instituting proceeding', ICJ, 29 December 2023, icj-cij.org.

11 Clothilde Mraffko, 'Gaza: New accounts of the "flour massacre"', *Le Monde*, 29 February 2024.

12 Julian Borger, 'Israel yet to provide evidence to back UNRWA 7 October attack claims – UN', *Guardian*, 1 March 2024.

13 United Nations, 'Independent review panel releases final report on UNRWA', 22 April 2024, news.un.org.

14 Neve Gordon and Muna Haddad, 'The road to famine in Gaza', *New York Review of Books*, 18 April 2024.

15 Raz Segal, 'A textbook case of genocide', *Jewish Currents*, 13 October 2023.

16 All quotes and references can be found in the document Republic of South Africa, 'Application instituting proceeding', ICJ, 29 December 2023, icj-cij.org.

17 Darryl Li, 'The charge of genocide', *Dissent Magazine*, 18 January 2024.

18 International Court of Justice, 'Order: Application of the Convention on the prevention and punishment of the crime of genocide in the Gaza Strip (South Africa v. Israel)', 26 January 2024.

19 'World reacts to ICJ interim ruling in Gaza genocide case against Israel', *Al Jazeera*, 26 January 2024.

20 France Diplomatie, 26 January 2024, diplomatie.gouv.fr.

21 United Nations, 'Security council again fails to adopt resolution demanding immediate humanitarian ceasefire in Gaza on account of veto by United States', 20 February 2024, press. un.org.

22 'Livraisons à Israël d'équipements pour mitrailleuses: la France entretient l'opacité', *Disclose*, 28 March 2024, and Nick Robertson, 'Democrats press Blinken on arms sales to Israel without congressional approval', *The Hill*, 29 January 2024.

23 Jean-Philippe Lefief, 'Israël: qui sont ses principaux fournisseurs d'armes?' *Le Monde*, 22 March 2024.

24 On 24 October 2023, visiting the Israeli prime minister, the French president called for the formation of an international military coalition against Hamas similar to that against the Islamic State. It was never put in place, the proposal having even been ignored by his interlocutor: Philippe Ricard, Louis Imbert et Piotr Smolar, 'Macron surprises leaders with proposal to "fight Hamas" with international coalition against IS', *Le Monde*, 25 October 2023. But the French air force took part, along with half a dozen other countries, in the operation against Iranian drones and missiles on 13 April 2023: Victor Goury-Laffont, 'Macron: France intercepted Iranian drones at "Jordan's request"', *Politico*, 15 April 2024.

25 Eyal Weizman, 'Three genocides', *London Review of Books*, 46 (8), 25 April 2024. The author, who has conducted research on the sites of the massacres in farms now owned by descendants of German soldiers, notes the 'curious historical coincidence' between the date of Germany's second hearing contesting the existence of a genocide perpetrated by the Israelis in Gaza before the ICJ, on 12 January 2024, and the commemoration of the 120th anniversary of the events that triggered the genocide perpetrated by the Germans against the Herero and Nama on 12 January 1904.

26 Donald Matthys, 'Namibia slams Germany's support of Israel against genocide claim', *The Namibian*, 14 January 2024.

27 DeNeen Brown, 'Why Namibia invoked a century-old German genocide in court', *Washington Post*, 20 January 2024. Remarkably, the massacre committed in Africa was known and even discussed in Palestine at the beginning of the twentieth century. The historian in Jewish studies Ron Naiweld told me that he translated a letter in Hebrew from a young Jewish worker, published on 12 June 1907 in the World Zionist Organization's weekly, *Ha-Olam*. In it the man mentions a conversation with an individual who, referring to the way the local Arab population was treated by the Jews at the time, asked him: 'What's the difference between us and the Germans who are now fighting Blacks in Africa?'

28 Amos Goldberg, 'Yes, it is a genocide', *The Palestine Project*, 18 April 2024, translated from Hebrew by Sol Salbe. The first lines of the text convey the emotion of this professor at the Hebrew University of Jerusalem: 'Yes, it is genocide. It is so difficult and painful to admit it, but despite all that, and despite all our efforts to think otherwise, after six months of brutal war we can no longer avoid this conclusion.'

Chapter 4

1 Human Rights Council, *Anatomy of a Genocide: Report of the Special Rapporteur on the Situation of Human Rights in the Palestinian Territories Occupied Since 1967*, United Nations, 25 March 2024.

2 Edgar Morin, 'Le progrès des connaissances a suscité une régression de la pensée', *Le Monde*, 22 January 2024.

3 Matthew Mpoke Bigg, 'Israel's UN ambassador criticized for wearing a yellow star of David', *New York Times*, 31 October 2023.

4 Gabriel Winant, 'On mourning and statehood', *Dissent Magazine*, 13 October 2023.

5 Dina Porat, 'Should we compare the Hamas assault to the Holocaust?', *Haaretz*, 23 October 2023.

6 Enzo Traverso, 'La guerre à Gaza brouille la mémoire de l'Holocauste', *Mediapart*, 5 November 2023.

7 Annie Karni, 'Schumer urges new leadership in Israel, calling Netanyahu an obstacle to peace', *New York Times*, 14 March 2024.

8 Didier Fassin, 'The rhetoric of denial: Contribution to an archive of the debate about mass violence in Gaza', *Journal of Genocide Research*, 5 February 2024.

9 André Perrin, '"Israël a le droit de se défendre, mais . . ." Les failles d'une rhétorique hypocrite', *Le Figaro*, 22 November 2023.

10 Jason Willick, 'We can't ignore the truth that Hamas uses human shields', *Washington Post*, 14 November 2023.

11 Avi Garfinkel, 'The Israeli army is still the most moral in the world', *Haaretz*, 26 December 2023.

12 Anthony Deutsch and Stephanie Van der Berg, 'What war crime laws apply to the Israel-Palestine conflict', *Reuters*, 16 November 2023.

13 Ben Burgis, 'The "human shields" defense of bombing Gaza's civilians is morally bankrupt', *Jacobin*, 20 November 2023.

14 Yaniv Kubovich and Michael Hauser Tov, 'Israeli army uses Palestinian civilians to inspect potentially booby-trapped tunnels in Gaza', *Haaretz*, 13 August 2024; Defense for Children International – Palestine section, '"They were trying to exterminate us": Palestinian children in Gaza tortured by Israeli military', *DCIP*, Ramallah, 21 August 2024.

15 Yuval Abraham, 'A "mass assassination factory." Inside Israel's calculated bombing of Gaza', +972, 30 November 2023.

16 Lee Mordechai, 'Documenting six months of Israeli war

crimes in Gaza', *Jacobin*, 17 April 2024. The Israeli historian has systematically collected information from multiple sources about the crimes committed by the IDF in Gaza, regularly updating what may constitute the most significant archive of the brutalization of Israeli society. He later published: 'Bearing Witness to the Israel-Gaza War', 18 June 2024.

17 United Nations, 'Mass graves in Gaza show victims' hands were tied, says UN rights office', *UN News*, 23 April 2024; and Federica Marsi, 'Gaza's mass graves: Is the truth being uncovered?', *Al Jazeera*, 11 May 2024.

18 Oren Ziv, '"I'm bored, so I shoot": The Israeli army's approval of free-for-all violence in Gaza', +972, 8 July 2024.

19 Melanie Stern and Liron Amir, 'We're not only here to fuck Hamas': How Israeli militarism took over online dating', *Haaretz*, 24 March 2024.

20 Anne Bernas, 'Guerre à Gaza. Ce que risquent les Franco-Israéliens auteurs d'exactions', *Radio France Internationale*, 22 March 2024. The racist video of the French military cheering for a massacre has gone viral: lnr-dz.com/2024/01/22/je-vous-emmene-a-ghaza.

21 Isaac Chotiner, 'The brutal conditions facing Palestinian prisoners', *New Yorker*, 21 March 2024.

22 Jonathan Ofir, '"We are the masters of the house": Israeli channels air snuff videos featuring systematic torture of Palestinians', *Mondoweiss*, 6 March 2024.

23 Hanin Majadli, 'Israel is hiding its draconian detention of Palestinians from the public', *Haaretz*, 13 June 2024.

24 Raja Abdulrahim, 'A Gaza doctor has died in Israeli custody, Palestinian groups say', *New York Times*, 3 May 2024.

25 International Holocaust Remembrance Alliance, 'Working definition of antisemitism', 26 May 2016, holocaustremembrance.com.

26 Chris McGreal, 'UN urged to reject antisemitism definition over misuse to shield Israel', *Guardian*, 24 April 2023, and

Abigail Bakan, Alejandro Paz, Anna Zalik and Deborah Cowen, 'Jewish scholars defend the right to academic freedom on Israel/Palestine', *The Conversation*, 12 April 2021.

27 Pankaj Mishra, 'The Shoah after Gaza', *London Review of Books*, 46 (6), 21 March 2024.

28 Jean Améry, 'The limits of solidarity: On diaspora Jewry's relationship to Israel', in *Essays on Antisemitism, Anti-Zionism and the Left*, ed. Marlene Gallner, Bloomington, Indiana University Press, 2021, pp. 74–7, 1st edition 1977.

29 Primo Levi, 'Se questo è uno Stato', *L'Espresso*, 30 September 1984, republished on the website Doppiozero, 28 November 2023, doppiozero.com.

30 'The Jerusalem Declaration on Antisemitism', jerusalem-declaration.org. Among the signatories, some have adopted radically different positioning after 7 October.

Chapter 5

1 Kennan Malik, 'Solidarity with Palestinians is not hate speech, whatever would-be censors may say', *Guardian*, 3 December 2023.

2 Laurent Fabius and Bernard Cazeneuve, 'France is not an antisemitic nation', *New York Times*, 10 July 2014.

3 Didier Fassin and Anne-Claire Defossez, 'L'honneur perdu du gouvernement français', *Libération*, 24 July 2014.

4 Louise Couvelaire, 'Antisémitisme: au dîner du CRIF, Macron promet des "actes tranchants"', *Le Monde*, 21 February 2019.

5 Soazig Le Nevé, 'Sciences Po s'embrase après une mobilisation pro-palestinienne, des insultes entendues et des versions contradictoires', *Le Monde*, 13 March 2024, and 'Sciences Po: la réponse agace des directeurs et des doyens après la "visite inopinée" de Gabriel Attal', *Le Monde*, 18 March 2024.

6 'Étudiant.es juif.ves à Sciences Po: nous ne serons pas instrumentalisé.es', *Mediapart*, 14 March 2024.

7 Guy Lodge, ' "No Other Land" review: A frank, devastating protest against Israel's West Bank occupation', *Variety*, 23 February 2024.

8 Alex Marshall, 'Criticism of Israel at Berlin Film Festival stirs antisemitism debate', *New York Times*, 27 February 2024.

9 Leo Sands, 'Israel filmmaker engulfed in backlash after anti-war speech in Berlin', *Washington Post*, 28 February 2024.

10 Anne-Françoise Hivert and Thomas Wieder, 'Greta Thunberg's stance splits the Fridays for Future climate movement', *Le Monde*, 18 November 2023.

11 Liza Featherstone, 'The most disingenuous attack on Greta Thunberg this year', *New Republic*, 21 December 2023.

12 Anaïs Condomines, 'Pourquoi le symbole des mains rouges, utilisé par des étudiants de Sciences-Po Paris en soutien à la Palestine, fait polémique?', *Libération*, 28 April 2024; 'Jerusalem marathon. Runners with fake blood on their hands call for hostage release deal', *Times of Israel*, 8 March 2024. The accusation of antisemitism relies on a dual displacement: the confiscation of a symbol with multiple meanings to retain only one, related to Israel as victim, and the translation of the murder of soldiers of an occupying army into the murder of Jews.

13 Yunnez Abzouz and Lucie Delaporte, 'Conflit israélo-palestinien. Une chape de plomb s'est abattue sur l'université française', *Mediapart*, 21 November 2023.

14 'Université Lyon 2: une conférence jugée pro-palestinienne annulée sur demande de la préfecture', *Le Progrès,* 30 January 2024; Clothilde Mraffko, 'In devastated Gaza, a photographer recounts the stories of the dead and displaced', *Le Monde*, 21 October 2023.

15 Loveday Morris and Kate Brady, 'In Germany's struggle against antisemitism, the arts are suffering', *Washington Post*, 22 December 2023.

16 Matt Fitzpatrick, 'As the war in Gaza continues, Germany's unstinting defense of Israel has unleashed a culture war that has just reached Australia', *Conversation*, 12 February 2024; Kate Connolly, 'German university rescinds Jewish American's job offer over pro-Palestinian letter', *Guardian*, 10 April 2024.

17 Jack Jeffery and Geir Moulson, 'Prominent surgeon says he was refused entry to Germany for pro-Palestinian conference', *Associated Press*, 12 April 2024; Mathias Thépot, 'Venu témoigner des bombardements à Gaza, le chirurgien palestinien Ghassan Abu Sittah est resté bloqué à Roissy', *Mediapart*, 4 May 2024. Professor Abu-Sittah is rector of the University of Glasgow.

18 Poll conducted between 10 and 17 November 2023 by the Middle East Scholar Barometer, criticalissues.umd.edu.

19 Kathryn Palmer, 'Punishments rise as student protests escalate', *Inside Higher Education*, 15 April 2024.

20 Lara Nour-Walton, 'Inside the Gaza solidarity encampment at Columbia University', *Nation*, 19 April 2024.

21 Steve Gorman, 'UCLA police chief reassigned following mob attack on pro-Palestinians protesters', *Reuters*, 23 May 2024.

22 Branko Marcetic, 'Last night's Palestine crackdown was authoritarian', *Jacobin*, 1 May 2024.

23 'Student protests against Israel's offensive in Gaza spread', *Le Monde*, 5 May 2024.

24 The human rights and legal aid organization Adalah, whose name means 'Justice' in Arabic, monitors numerous cases involving attacks on freedom of expression: 'Crackdown on freedom of speech of Palestinian citizens in Israel', adalah.org.

25 Survey conducted by Ipsos for the University of Maryland from 21 to 27 June 2024: criticalissues.umd.edu.

26 Henri Seckel, 'Antisémitisme: 1 518 actes recensés en France depuis le 7 octobre, peu de condamnations', *Le*

Monde, 15 November 2023; Nonna Mayer, 'Les stéréo-types antisémites gardent un certain impact dans une petite partie de la gauche', *Le Monde*, 10 November 2023.

27 Kanishka Singh, 'Anti-Muslim Incidents Jump in US Amid Israel-Gaza War', *Reuters*, 29 January 2024.

28 'France: Forte hausse des actes anti-musulmans en 2023, dont plus de la moitié depuis le 7 octobre', *Middle East Eye*, 27 February 2024.

Chapter 6

1 Ofri Ilany, 'The mass killing in Gaza will poison Israeli souls forever', *Haaretz*, 21 March 2024.

2 Didier Fassin, *De l'inégalité des vies*, Paris, Fayard-Collège de France, 2020.

3 During Operation Cast Lead, 1,398 Palestinians, including 1,391 in Gaza, were killed, and also 9 Israelis, including 3 civilians. Statistics on the number of Palestinian civilians are difficult to establish and subject to controversy. If we use B'Tselem's definition, that is, Palestinians killed by the Israeli army when they were not taking part in activities and were not, in principle, being targeted, 764 civilians were killed, including 318 minors and 108 women: statistics.btselem.org. Unlike the Israeli army, which provides unspecified numbers, and considers all adult males to be terrorists, B'Tselem indicates each identity, including name, age and sex, and the circumstances of the victim's death.

4 During Operation Protective Edge, 2,251 Palestinians were killed – 789 combatants and 1,462 civilians, including 299 women and 551 children – as well as 76 Israelis – 70 soldiers and 6 civilians: digitallibrary.un.org. The Israeli army gives similar figures for the total number of deaths, i.e. 2,125, but grossly underestimates the number of civilians – 761.

5 Merlyn Thomas, Jake Horton and Benedict Garman, 'Israel-Gaza: Checking Israel's claim to have killed 10,000 Hamas fighters', BBC, 29 February 2024.

6 'Contrary to Israel's claims, 9 out of 10 of those killed in Gaza are civilians', *Euro-Mediterranean Human Rights Monitor*, 5 December 2023.

7 Figures provided for Gaza by the United Nations for all deaths recorded – 32,623 on 6 April 2024 – and by Save the Children regarding children alone – 13,800 on 4 April 2024: reliefweb.int/report and savethechildren.org.

8 Raphael Cohen, 'Why the October 7 attack was not Israel's 9/11', *Lawfare*, 12 November 2023.

9 We Are Not Numbers, wearenotnumbers.org.

10 Eitan Barak, 'Under cover of darkness: Israeli Supreme Court and the use of human lives as bargaining chips', *International Journal of Human Rights*, 3 (3), 1999.

11 Jonathan Kuttab, 'The International Criminal Court's failure to hold Israel accountable', Arab Center Washington, 12 September 2023.

12 Harry Davies, Bethan McKernan, Yuval Abraham and Meron Rapoport, 'Spying, hacking and intimidation: Israel's nine-year "war" on the ICC exposed', *Guardian*, 28 May 2024.

13 Nadera Shalhoub-Kevorkian, 'The occupation of the senses: The prosthetic and aesthetic of state terror', *British Journal of Criminology*, 57 (6), 2017: 1279–300. The author, who is professor at the Hebrew University of Jerusalem, was suspended by her institution in March 2024 for her criticisms of the war on Gaza, then detained by Israeli police, before being released and reinstated.

14 Haggai Matar, 'Police spray putrid water on Palestinian homes, schools', +972, 15 November 2014.

15 Scott Wilson, 'In Gaza, lives shaped by drones', *Washington Post*, 3 December 2011.

16 Saree Makdisi, 'No human being can exist', *n+1*, 25 October 2023.

17 Acrimed, 'Naufrage et asphyxie du débat public', 20 December 2023, acrimed.org; Blast, 'Un naufrage médiatique sans précédent', 31 March 2024, youtube.com.

18 Excerpts from news broadcast on the national public radio.

19 Shrouq Aïla, 'Inside the Nuseirat massacre: this carnage I saw during Israel's hostage rescue', *Intercept*, 10 June 2024; Gideon Levy, 'Why did Israel conceal hundreds of Gazans' deaths in "perfect" hostage rescue operation?', *Haaretz*, 12 June 2024. The day after the attack, the coverage of the happy news on the Israeli side lasted twenty-four times longer than the evocation of the tragic reality on the Palestinian side, even though it was already known. Meanwhile, the French and US presidents were rejoicing at the release of the four Israeli hostages, without a word for the hundreds of Palestinian civilian victims.

20 Human Rights Watch, *Meta's Broken Promises: Systemic Censorship of Palestine Content on Instagram and Facebook*, 21 December 2023: hrw.org/report. Of 1,050 contents censored on Facebook and Instagram and verified by Human Rights Watch, 1,049 were peaceful.

21 Livia Wick, *Sumud: Birth, Oral History and Persisting in Palestine*, Syracuse, Syracuse University Press, 2022.

22 India McTaggart, 'BBC reporters accuse it of favouritism towards Israel', *Telegraph*, 23 November 2023.

23 Jeremy Scahill, 'Leaked NYT Gaza memo tells journalists to avoid words "genocide", "ethnic cleansing" and "occupied territories"', *Intercept*, 15 April 2024.

24 Adam Johnson and Othman Ali, 'Coverage of Gaza war in the New York Times and other major newspapers heavily favored Israel, analysis shows', *Intercept*, 9 January 2024.

25 Laura Wagner and Will Sommer, 'Hundreds of journalists sign letter protesting coverage of Israel', *Washington Post*, 9 November 2023.

26 Tariq Kenney-Shawa, 'Israel's disinformation apparatus:

A key weapon in its arsenal', *Al-Shabaka. The Palestinian Policy Network*, 12 March 2024.

27 The corrections made at the beginning of May 2024 by the United Nations to the proportion of women and children officially killed in Gaza, by only taking into account the data for which civil status information existed, gave rise to malicious insinuations and sarcastic comments, which made no mention of the fact that, if the statistics are increasingly difficult to validate, it is because the Israeli army has destroyed the hospitals that collected them and the communication channels that transmitted them: Graeme Wood, 'The UN's Gaza statistics make no sense', *Atlantic*, 17 May 2024.

28 Ryan Grim and Prem Thakker, 'Biden's conspiracy theory about Gaza casualty numbers unravels upon inspection', *Intercept*, 31 October 2023.

29 Benjamin Huynh, Elizabeth Chin and Paul Spiegel, 'No evidence of inflated mortality reporting from the Gaza Ministry of Health', *Lancet*, 6 December 2023.

30 Stephanie Savell, *How Death Outlives War: The Reverberating Impact of the Post-9/11 Wars on Human Health*, Watson Institute, Brown University, 15 May 2023.

31 Rasha Khatib, Martin McKee and Salim Yusuf, 'Counting the dead in Gaza: difficult but essential', *Lancet*, 404, 20 July 2024. Based on the 37,396 deaths from the official data of the first eight months of the war and using the 'conservative estimate of four indirect deaths per one direct death', the three experts conclude that the final number could be at least 186,0000 victims, that is, 7.9 per cent of the population.

32 William Marx, 'Ce qu'Œdipe et Antigone nous disent de la crise au Proche-Orient', *Le Monde*, 15 November 2023.

33 According to François Hollande, interviewed on 7 February 2024 on national public television, there is an almost ontological difference between 'the victims of terrorism and the victims of war', which, in his view,

justifies paying national tribute to the former, who are Franco-Israeli, but not the latter, who are Franco-Palestinian: francetvinfo.fr/monde.

34 Judith Butler, *Frames of War: When Is Life Grievable?* London, Verso, 2009, pp. 24, 31, 38.

35 Vivian Yee, Iyad Abuheweilia, Abu Bakr Bashir and Ameera Harouda, 'Gaza shadow death toll: Bodies buried beneath the rubble', *New York Times*, 23 March 2024; Ruth Michaelson, 'UN rights chief "horrified" by reports of mass graves at two Gaza hospitals', *Guardian*, 23 April 2024; Stéphanie Latte Abdallah, *Des morts en guerre. Rétention des corps et figures du martyr en Palestine*, Paris, Karthala, 2022.

36 Louis Imbert, 'The Israeli left's existential crisis', *Le Monde*, 3 November 2023.

37 Didier Fassin, 'The inequality of Palestinian lives', *Berlin Review*, 1 (1), 2 February 2024.

38 Nicolas Truong, 'La guerre entre Israël et le Hamas fracture le monde intellectuel', *Le Monde*, 8 December 2023.

Chapter 7

1 Esmat Elhalaby, 'Toward an intellectual history of genocide in Gaza: Destruction begins with ideas', *Baffler*, 27 March 2024.

2 Vladimir Bortun, 'How academia failed the test of the war in Gaza', *Jacobin*, 27 July 2024.

3 Ivar Ekeland, 'Échange entre l'Aurdip et France Universités concernant la guerre à Gaza', 17 November 2023. AURDIP is the Association of academics for the respect of international law in Palestine: aurdip.org.

4 Catherine Hass, 'Si la guerre est sans but, elle est nécessairement sans fin', *Mediapart*, 20 March 2024. The Institut du monde arabe, in Paris, organized in the spring

of 2023 an art exposition titled 'Ce que la Palestine apporte au monde': imarabe.org.

5 Jamie Dettmer, 'Israel's trauma was compounded by talk of an existential threat', *Politico*, 27 November 2023.

6 Muhammad Maqdsi, 'Charter of the Islamic Resistance Movement (Hamas) of Palestine', *Journal of Palestine Studies*, 22 (4), 1993: 122–34.

7 Khaled Hroub, 'A newer Hamas? The Revised Charter', *Journal of Palestine Studies*, 46 (4), 2017: 100–11.

8 Hamas leader Ismail Haniyeh, who had opened the way to a two-state solution in his 2017 statement, was assassinated on 30 July 2024: 'A Hamas leader killed in Iran during visit', *The New York Times,* 30 July 2024.

9 Likud Party, 'The right of the Jewish people to the land of Israel', *Original Party Platform*, 1977, jewishvirtuallibrary. org.

10 Amnesty International, *Israel's Occupation: 50 Years of Dispossession,* 7 June 2017, amnesty.org.

11 Human Rights Council, *The Question of Palestine,* United Nations, 27 February – 31 March 2023.

12 Nadia Abu El-Haj, 'Zionism's political unconscious', Verso Blog, 17 November 2023.

13 Rashid Khalidi, 'It's time to confront Israel's Version of "From the river to the sea"', *Nation,* 22 November 2023.

14 United Nations, *General Assembly. Twenty-ninth session*, Official Records, 13 November 1974.

15 A Land for All, *Two States, One Homeland*, alandforall. org.

16 World Health Organization, 'Six months of war leave Al-Shifa hospital in ruins', 6 April 2024, who.int.

17 World Health Organization, 'Famine in Gaza is imminent, with immediate and long-term health consequences', 18 March 2024, who.int.

18 Interesting is the U-turn by the French government which, unlike the US and UK governments, has publicly given its

support to the jurisdiction in The Hague: icc-cpi.int/news/statement-icc.

19 Daniel Estrin, 'A State Department official warns Israel of "major" reputational damage in Gaza war', NPR, 22 March 2024.

20 John Hudson, 'US signs off on more bombs, warplanes to Israel', *Washington Post*, 29 March 2024.

21 Stéphanie Le Bars, 'The vast majority of Israel's Jewish population don't want to see the Gazans' suffering', *Le Monde*, 7 April 2024.

22 Editorial, 'The brutalisation of Israel is well underway. If we do not act, its collapse is only a matter of time', *Haaretz,* 7 June 2024. The Hebrew version used the phrase 'bestialization of Israel'.

23 Gideon Levy, 'The reaction to a Gazan doctor's release reveals the troubling state of Israeli society', *Haaretz*, 3 July 2024. Most of the other doctors released during this period had been tortured and starved for months, and their bodies bore the scars of their mistreatment, which had left them destroyed and unrecognisable human beings.

24 Anna Gordon, 'New polling shows how much global support Israel has lost', *Time,* 17 January 2024.

25 Aluf Benn, 'Israel's self-destruction: Netanyahu, the Palestinians and the price of neglect', *Foreign Affairs*, 7 February 2024.

26 'Rwanda: pour Emmanuel Macron, la France "aurait pu arrêter le génocide", mais n'en a "pas eu la volonté"', *Le Monde*, 4 April 2024. In view of the political reactions against this statement, and perhaps understanding the legal risk of a complaint for complicity in genocide, the French president finally withdrew it from his communication to the authorities in Kigali, who did not even release it.

27 Mona Chollet, 'Le conflit qui rend fou. Devant la catastrophe en Israël-Palestine', *La Méridienne*, 27 October 2023.

28 Thomas Wieder, 'The war between Hamas and Israel takes

Germany back to its own historical responsibility', *Le Monde*, 10 November 2023.

29 Pankaj Mishra, 'Memory failure', *London Review of Books*, 46 (1), 4 January 2024.

30 George Prochnik, Eyal Weizman and Emily Dische-Becker, 'Once again, Germany defines who is a Jew', *Granta*, 23 November 2023.

31 Daniel Boguslaw and Ken Klippenstein, 'The secret alliance that defended Israel from Iran attack', *The Intercept*, 18 April 2024. Iraq, Jordan and Saudi Arabia, as well as, indirectly, Qatar, Kuwait, Bahrain and the UAE, participated in the operation with the United States, France and Britain. To avoid escalation, the Iranians had prewarned these countries of their action.

32 Gilles Deleuze and Elias Sanbar, 'Les Indiens de Palestine', *Libération*, 8–9 May 1982. Translated at versobooks.com.

33 Bernard Norlain, 'Israël et la bombe. L'histoire du nucléaire israélien', *Revue Défense nationale*, 837, 2021: 127–32.

34 'How much aid does the US give to Israel', *USA Facts*, 12 October 2023.

35 Jonathan Masters and Will Merrow, 'US aid to Israel in four charts', *Council on Foreign Relations*, 11 April 2024.

36 Jean-Pierre Filiu, 'How Benjamin Netanyahu became the self-proclaimed leader of the "civilized world"', *Le Monde*, 29 October 2023.

37 Catherine Caruso, 'After House speaker Mike Johnson pushed through Israel aid package, AIPAC cash came flowing in', *The Intercept*, 20 January 2024, and Akela Lacy, 'The left is finally building a response to AIPAC', *The Intercept*, 11 March 2024.

38 Vincent Geisser, 'L'islamophobie en France au regard du débat européen', in Rémi Leveau and Khadidja Mohsen-Finan, eds, *Les Musulmans de France et d'Europe*, Paris, CNRS Éditions, 2005, pp. 59–79. For the United States, the genealogy is different, since they did not have the same

colonial interactions with Arabs and Muslims, but the Six-Day War was a turning point, or at least revealed prejudices against the latter: Edward Said, 'The Arab portrayed', *The Arab World*, 1967, republished in Ibrahim Abu-Lughod ed., *The Arab-Israeli Confrontation of June 1967: an Arab Perspective*, Evanston: Northwestern University Press, 1970, pp. 1–9.

39 Marc-Olivier Behrer, 'Le "grand remplacement". Généalogie d'un complotisme caméléon', *Le Monde*, 25 August 2022; ACLU, *Timeline of the Muslim Ban,* Washington, aclu-wa.org; Cady Lang, 'Who gets to wear a headscarf? The complex history behind France's latest hijab controversy', *Time*, 19 May 2021; Arsalan Iftikhar, 'German ministry issues 400-page report on islamophobia', *Bridge*, Georgetown University, 1 February 2024; Ugo Santkin, 'Nationalité belge retirée à des enfants de parents palestiniens: "Une décision sans précédent et profondément discriminante"', *Le Soir*, 7 December 2023.

40 Laurence Alexandrowicz, 'Les associations dénoncent un traitement différent des réfugiés afghans et ukrainiens', *Euronews*, 11 May 2022.

41 Karishma Mehrotra, 'India's Mideast rethink: From a Palestine stamp to a "Modi-Bibi bromance"', *Washington Post*, 18 November 2023.

42 Uriya Shavit, '"Muslims are the new Jews" in the West: Reflections on contemporary parallelisms', in Armin Lange, Kerstin Mayerhofer, Dina Porat and Lawrence Schiffman, eds, *Confronting Antisemitism in Modern Media, the Legal and Political Worlds*, Berlin, De Gruyter, 2021.

43 Ifop, 'L'État de l'opinion à l'égard du racisme et de l'antisémitisme', March 2021, ifop.com.

44 On the National Rally, see Olivier Faye, 'Serge Klarsfeld, le chasseur de nazis qui n'a plus peur du RN', *Le Monde*, 16 December 2023. But the historic advocate of the victims of the 'Shoah' is not the only one to say he prefers the Rally to

France Unbound: Youmni Kezzouf, 'Face à la drague du RN, la communauté juive s'interroge', *Mediapart*, 26 November 2023. With regard to the Reconquest party, see Louis Imbert, 'Élection présidentielle 2022. Les Français d'Israël ont voté à plus de 50% pour Éric Zemmour', *Le Monde*, 12 April 2022. The Reconquest candidate won 53 per cent of the vote in Israel, albeit with a low turnout, while in France, in areas with a high Jewish population, he also achieved high scores, as in Sarcelles, where he topped 35 per cent in so-called 'Little Jerusalem', five times more than at national level: Lucas Jakobowicz, 'Présidentielle 2022: Oui, la religion détermine le vote', *Décideurs Magazine*, 19 April 2022.

45 Chaim Gans, 'Storms in the Negev 2023, or, Why is history mocking Israel', *Israel Studies*, 29 (1), 2024: 62–73.

Chapter 8

1 Heidi Mogstad, 'Gaza is not a humanitarian crisis: On self-defense, depoliticizing language and contextualization', Bergen, Christian Michelsen Institute, 2023, cmi.no/publications/8976. The nightmare in Gaza is more than a humanitarian crisis, the UN secretary general powerfully stated. 'It is a crisis of humanity': press.un.org.

2 Pierre Vidal-Naquet, 'Qui sont les assassins de la mémoire ?', in *Réflexions sur le génocide. Les Juifs, la mémoire et le présent*, volume 3, Paris, La Découverte, 1995.

3 Didier Fassin, *Sciences sociales par temps de crise*, Paris, Fayard-Collège de France, 2023.

4 ICJ, *Legal Consequences Arising from the Policies and Practices of Israel in the Occupied Palestinian Territory, including East Jerusalem*, 19 July 2024: icj-cij.org.

5 Barbara Cassin, ' "Removing the perpetuity of hatred": On South Africa as a model example', *International Review of the Red Cross*, 88 (862), 2006: 235–44.

6 Didier Fassin, *When Bodies Remember: Experiences and Politics of AIDS in South Africa*, Berkeley, University of California Press, 2007.

7 Raja Shehadeh, *What Does Israel Fear from Palestine?* New York, Other Press, 2024.

8 Reinhart Koselleck, *L'Expérience de l'histoire*, trans. Alexandre Escudier, Paris, Gallimard-Seuil, 1997, p. 239.

9 Walter Benjamin, 'On the Concept of History', IX, trans. Harry Zohn, in *Selected Writings: Volume 4, 1938–1940*, Howard Eiland and Michael W. Jennings, eds., Cambridge, Mass., Harvard University Press, 2003, p. 392.

10 Jehad Abusalim, 'Refaat Alareer was a brilliant poet and intellectual – he was also my teacher', *Nation*, 15 December 2023.

11 Refaat Alareer, 'If I Must Die', *In These Times*, 27 December 2023. The title and the first verse are a reminiscence of, and a tribute to, the poem 'If We Must Die' by the Jamaican American writer Claude McKay, who wrote it in 1919 in the context of the Red Summer, during which Black people were the victims of racist attacks that left hundreds dead. Flying kites is a popular activity for Palestinian children, and even at the height of the war, some of them managed to rediscover the pleasure between two exoduses or two bombings: Ruwaida Amer, 'Kites fill Rafah's skies, a symbol of hope amid Israel's war on Gaza', *Al Jazeera*, 20 February 2024. It is indeed a symbol of hope, but perhaps also an ultimate resistance, tiny and decisive, in the face of the plan to annihilate them.